THE GOSPEL MESSAGE:
AS WE NEVER HEARD BEFORE

Leonard T. Wolcott

THE GOSPEL MESSAGE: AS WE NEVER HEARD BEFORE
Copyright © 2006 by Leonard T. Wolcott

Some rights reserved. Creative Commons Attribution-NonCommercial-ShareAlike 2.0 License. Copyright and License apply to text only and not to images or illustrations used herein. For information contact Fairfield Glade United Methodist Church, 213 Westchester Drive, Fairfield Glade, Tennessee 38558.

Edited by Paul C. Wennermark

ISBN 978-1-84728-374-0

Writing for all ages, Dr. Wolcott's numerous published works authored or co-authored include: First and Second Chronicles, Hebrews, Introduction l'étude du Nouveau Testament et de Son Message, La Iglesia en el Mundo, Meditations on Ephesians, New Testament Odyssey, Religions Around the World, Through the Moongate, Twelve Modern Disciples, We Go Forward!, and Wilderness Rider.

Grateful acknowledgment is given for illustration graphics obtained from Web site www.stmarycoptorthodox.org and used on chapter title pages.

The graphic used on the book cover and title page is a South Italian (perhaps Benevento), Ivory Plaque with Agnus Dei on a Cross between Emblems of the Four Evangelists, 975-1000 AD. The Metropolitan Museum of Art, Gift of J. Pierpont Morgan, 1917, (17.190.38) Photograph © 1999 The Metropolitan Museum of Art.

Preface

In 2004, I began to write brief reviews of each previous week's Bible study. These reviews were not commentaries on the Bible passages so much as thoughts arising from some of our class discussions. That is why they came to take a more free, poetic or rhythmic form. Almost every verse in the Gospels has special meaning. If I had tried to write on each verse, I thought, "I suppose that the world itself could not contain them."

Unbeknownst to me, Don Sutherland, perhaps others also, began to save these reviews. Finally, I received a formal request to permit their publication. Paul Wennermark became the careful editor, selecting the reviews and putting them in one of the five sections of the book. Some of the reviews are of verses found in one Gospel only. Many are found in two or more. I am so grateful to them, and I hope many others will be, for letting me and our Bible study group share thoughts and faith in the Word. It is the Truth that has inspired and guided the generations who have loved God the Father of our Lord Jesus Christ.

Perhaps more verse may be added in the future. Perhaps you, the reader, may want to write in your own words and thoughts that come to you as you read the Bible.

Leonard T. Wolcott

Illustrations - The Four Evangelists*

The illustrations used on the cover and chapter title pages come from art of the early Middle Ages. Christian tradition has long connected the authors of the four canonical Gospels (Matthew, Mark, Luke, John) with the four "living creatures" that surround God's throne, as in Rev. 4:7. The cover icon depicts in symbolic form the four writers of the Gospels surrounding the Lamb of God: Matthew by the winged man, Mark by the winged lion, Luke by the winged ox, and John by the eagle. These creatures are also suggested in the vision of Ezekiel (Ezek. 1:10).

ST. MATTHEW: Matthew is called the divine man, since he teaches about the human nature of Christ and his version of the gospel begins with Jesus paternal genealogy.
ST. MARK: Mark is called the winged lion, since he informs us of the royal dignity of Christ and his version of the gospel begins: "The voice of one crying in the wilderness," suggesting the roar of the lion.
ST. LUKE: Luke is called the winged ox, since he deals with the sacrificial aspects of Christ's life and his version of the gospel begins with a scene in the temple.
ST. JOHN: John is called the rising eagle, since his gaze pierces so far into the mysteries of Heaven and his version of the gospel begins with a lofty prologue that is a poem of the Word become flesh.
   *See www.metropolitonmuseum.com and www.stmarycoptorthodox.org/

Foreword

A lifetime of living with the gospels reveals their essence in these poems by Leonard T. Wolcott. Each one brings focus and illumination and offers comfort, challenge, and hope in easily grasped word and image.

Dr. Wolcott places all of the great questions of life under the light of the gospel in this splendid collection of poems. Who is God? Who am I? Why am I here? Where am I going? Where is Creation headed? Again and again I was surprised and blessed by the truth revealed in just a few carefully crafted words of poetry. Here is a wonderful companion to the Bible. In it you will find the essence of the four gospels in language and image that will make your heart sing, your soul rejoice, and will lead you into new paths of discipleship.
Rueben P. Job, Bishop, United Methodist Church

Dr. Wolcott has taken a very creative approach to looking at some of the most critical passages of scripture. This book can be used as collateral reading for any Bible study program. It challenges one to think about what you are being asked to do as a Christian.
William Morris, Bishop, United Methodist Church

It is hoped that the reader of this book will find the organization of poems in sequence by Gospel book, chapter, and verse to be most helpful. Note that many poems will have multiple and parallel scripture references. You are encouraged to locate these poems by parallel scripture verses using the index at the rear of this book.

Members of Dr. Wolcott's Sunday school class feel blessed by one small but glorious aspect of his teaching ministry. The many poems that he presented as a review of previous week's studies, helped bring alive the message of the Gospel. Nowhere else have we encountered a Bible commentary written in a rhythmic prose and poetry as these works of Dr. Wolcott. We felt compelled to provide a wider dissemination of his gift to the community of believers in Fairfield Glade, Tennessee and beyond. May all glory be to God, as you enjoy <u>The Gospel: As We Never Heard Before</u>.
Paul Wennermark, Editor

Contents

Preface 3
Illustrations - The Four Evangelists* 4
Foreword 5

CHAPTER 1

BOOK OF MATTHEW

The Great Drama 12
A Voice, an Event, in the Wilderness 13
The Messenger of Light 14
Practical Christianity 15
Waiting 16
The Sermon on the Mount and the Plain 17
Salt 18
Prayer 19
Thy Kingdom Come—The Blessed 21
On Treasure and Trust 23
Judge Not? 25
The Way 26
Call to Arms 27
Jesus and the Disciples, Apostles 28
He Told Them Stories 29
Transfiguration 30
Forgive 31
Never Say the Day Was Wasted 32
The Wedding Feast 33
Answer to the Herodians 34
Woe Is Me 35
Jesus In Tears 36
Ready for the Love-Feast? 38
The Great Investment 39
Agony 40
Joy 41
Judas of Kerioth 42

CHAPTER 2
BOOK OF MARK

Among the Many	44
Dare We Follow?	45
Beatitude	46
Capernaum	47
Alone	48
The Galilean Prophet	49
Jesus' Family	50
Yet He Loved Them	51
Who? Where? How?	52
In the Synagogue at Nazareth	53
The Rule of Love	54
The Rich Ruler	55
Sacrifice of the Servant	57
He Comes	59
Authority	60
On the Way to Jerusalem	61
Live to God	63
How Should We Live?	64
For Pharisees and Scribes, and Rulers and All of Them and Us	65
The Widow's Mite	66
The House of God	66
Rejoice	67
Troubled Yet Steadfast	68
Gethsemane	69
The Finish	70
Mary Magdalene	71

CHAPTER 3
BOOK OF LUKE

Our Last, But Lasting Message	74
The Word and the Touch	75
Kingdom Disciples	76
Cost and Courage	77
Transfiguration	78
The Seventy	79
Loving-Kindness	80
Teach Us to Pray	81
Help Us Pray	82
Father	83
…and speaking of Beelzebub	84
What Is Religion?	84
Signs	85
Clean	86
The Moral Zealots	87
Beware the Leaven of the Pharisees	88
Contrasts - Discipleship vs	89
The Company of Disciples	90
God Loves Them	91
What's Your Hurry?	92
The Great Invitation	93
God's Love for the Sinner	94
Who Is Your Master?	95
We Enter Now Your Kingdom	96
Greatness	97
Your Servants	98
Who God Justifies	99
A Few Words about a Little Man	100
The Missing Covenant	101
Barabbas	102
Gospel Postscript	103

CHAPTER 4
BOOK OF JOHN

Thank You, John	106
Jesus	107
Prologue to the Gospel of John	108
The Messiah Is Found	109
The Call to Follow	109
Waiting His Word, Willing His Will	110
Nicodemus	111
Snapshots in Samaria	112
There Came a Woman (of Samaria)	113
At the Sheep Gate	114
The Father Loves The Son	115
Testimony	116
By Himself	116
The Foolish Crowd	117
Afraid?	118
Disciples' Prayer	119
Divine Intent	120
Are You Blind?	121
Sin No More	122
Truth	123
One Thing I Know!	124
Jesus Wept	126
End Days	127
That Day	128
Yet A Little While	129
His Word	130
The Commandment's Commission	131
Connection	132
You Are My Friends	133
The First Day	133
Do You Not Know That I Have Power?	134

CHAPTER 5
RANDOM THOUGHTS

The Synoptic Gospels – I 136
The Synoptic Gospels – II 137
Tabernacled Questions 138
Templed Questions 138
Tabernacle and Temple 138
The Via Dolorosa 139
Hesed (Chesedh) 140
Riddle From the Gospels 141
Thoughts on the Lord's Prayer 142
One Will Come 143
Neighbor 144
Martha, Mary 145
Jesus Wonders 146

Scripture Index 149

CHAPTER 1

BOOK OF MATTHEW

The Great Drama
(Matthew 02:1, 10, 11; Luke 02:8-15)

A stink—dirty manger—a helpless baby

A blood nasty cross—a defenseless victim
These the parameters of the Eternal's sure kindness
The Creator appearing within His creation
Ultimate power in ultimate weakness
Unapproachable God in intimate closeness
The word of His love in human expression.

The wise came to wonder, amazement in splendor
But the poor, the unlettered, those burdened with labor
It is they hear the angels, the joy and the singing,
It is they bear the message:
Peace to all the earth's people
It is they, the God-pleased
Who will divine goodness.

It is in these natal stories of Jesus,
We see a dramatization of what He was,
And of what He taught
And most of all of what He did
In demonstrating God's righteousness.

A Voice, an Event, in the Wilderness
(Matthew 03:1-3, 13-4:1)

The news spread far and wide
>About the preacher in the desert,
>About the herald of the day of the Lord.

From far away they came and from nearby
To hear His words, in hope and fear
To wash away their sins, yet not alone
To escape the wrath of God
As to be ready for the messiah who would come.

Among the many there came one
(But who would know Him?)
For baptism—and the baptizer gasped,
"You! Not you by me. I need baptism by you!"

But this one who came, like all the others,
>Descended into the waters

And He saw, like a dove of pure beauty,
>A spirit of peace alight on Him.

And He heard a voice no man could speak:
"This is my beloved son in whom I am well pleased.
The semblance of my love."

Who could this stranger be?
What would He do?
What would He say?

He walked away.
Divinely present, humanly weak. He walked away.
Into the wilderness.

The Messenger of Light
(Matthew 03:1-12; John 01:6-7)

'There was a man sent from God…'
    Why was He here?
    Bearing witness to the light,
To point to the light that shows the way
That was why He was here: to show the way
      Before He went away.

They killed Him. They often kill the one who shows the way.
But the one who shows the way does what He is sent to do.
He suffers with joy
On a busy street or in a palace or a slum
Or on some gloaming road at dusk.

Why am I here?
What the purpose, what the meaning?
To show the scintillating sparkling sight
Of God's redeeming light.

Sent from God! Are we?
Testimonies of His life, then,
Overjoyed, returning back to Him who is the Way.

Practical Christianity
(Matthew 03:7-10)

Its roots are in the Hebrew prophets, spokesmen for God.

Through the prophets God says to His people:
"I chose you.
I promised to take care of you,
Asking you to obey My law, to do My will.
My law is the enactment of My righteousness.
My righteousness is reliably and always to do right by My people,
The people I have created,
Called, chosen, and promised to care for.
But you do not keep your part of the covenant.
    You disobeyed My law,
    You rebelled against My righteousness.
    You did not do right by others.
        I am angry with you
    I judge you, condemn you. I will punish you…
Unless you return to Me, and seek Me,
And do My will of righteous action.
Then I will come to you,
    And rescue you,   and restore you
And you will truly be My people, doing My will,
    Reflecting Me among the nations."

Waiting
(Matthew 04:17;Luke 02:25-38; John 03:2-3)

Devoutly many waited, like Simeon and Anna.

They prayed and they waited for the Great Day to come,
For the reign of God, the Messianic time, the life of perfection.
They waited in hope, not knowing how to live it.

Fervently many worked it. Like the Pharisees, the zealous.
They kept all the rules; they protected the doctrines,
And to please the Lord, they cast out all sinners.
They waited for God, not knowing how to love Him.

Then came this country peasant, the strong and humble Jesus
Who said, "Stop your waiting, for the Great Day has come.
Here is the Reign of God! Turn 'round and come on in.
Take care of the suffering, visit the sick, welcome the stranger."

Now this is the Kingdom, the proof is in living it.
Peace and goodwill is in love and forgiving.
Here's the House of God, reconciling friend and enemy.
Our joy is fulfilled in knowing how to share it.

The Sermon on the Mount and the Plain
(Matthew 05-7; Luke 06:20-49)

Oh, for the good life!
Moved with compassion, in loving-kindness.
Jesus healed the sick, restored the outcasts and the distressed,
Brought new life even to the dead, and gave the weary rest.
What is the good life?
Jesus told stories to describe it,
Illustrations from the common life,
Full of bright surprises, charmingly uncomfortable.
How live the good life?
We said, "Master, we want to be with you,
Go where you go, do what you do!"
He said, "Are you able?"
This, He said, is the good life:
It is, even though poor and hungry,
Sorrowing, despised, and ill-treated, always
  To be gentle and kind.
    Pure in heart, making peace,
      Boldly just, persistent in right-doing.
        And in all of this, rejoicing.
He said, it is to be a light in the world, a seasoning.
It is to be pulsed by the heart of God's will and God's law.
To be caring, not killing,
Loving, not lusting,
Faithful, not swearing,
Returning good for evil.
It is giving, not getting,
Praying, believing,
Cheerfully sharing,
Single-minded, committed, - one focus, one goal,
Trusting, so untroubled,
Not wrongfully judging, but rightly discerning,
Thoughtful for others.
It is not self-indulgence but disciplined probity.
No self-deception in the practice of goodness.
No frivolous folly, but deep-founded action.
These are the measures and the marks of the good life…

Salt
(Matthew 05:13)

"They," of some it has been said,
"Are the salt of the earth"…
Who give to life a seasoning,
A joyous savor, value, worth.

That is why, our Lord once said,
We are here just to care,
To counter worldly treasoning,
To show God's kindness everywhere.

Church, can it be truly said,
Is the practice of peace,
Forgiving and, with reasoning,
Sharing a love that will not cease?

Prayer
(Matthew 06:5-15)

Prayer *is an appeal to God.*
We at the center, calling God to attend us. But more…

Religious prayer is contact with God
Who is, as He was, and always will be: above us, beyond us but also…

Christian prayer is conversation with a personal God
Who, always present, is close beside us,
    incomprehensible Infinity, comprehendible within our finity.

Prayer is directing our thoughts to God,
God, not we ourselves at the center of our attention,
    we move from anxious clamor to expectant listening.

God is our Father, and we are His children
    (not just my Father and not just your Father, but *ours* together)
God our Father,
    Is greater than all His creation and all His creatures.

We have a request to make of God our Father,
It is the primary request of the Christian disciple.
It is a request that His rule, His realm,
His great purpose be realized:
    "Thy kingdom come,"

That not our desires but His will be done.
In the perfection we call "Heaven."
His will be truly done.
We yearn that it be perfectly done on earth,
Among us in our time.

Continued

"Feed us!", eagerly we pray. "with the bread of life.
That we might live by trust,
You, God, provide for us."

"Forgive us for the wrong we've done
As we forgive those who have wronged us."
(*For a forgiving attitude opens our hearts*
　　for God's forgiving love.)

"And please do not bring us to a test
　　We cannot bear
But save us from the evil one."

Thy Kingdom Come—The Blessed
(Matthew 06:9-15; Matthew 05:1-12)

Daily we pray
    "Thy Kingdom come!"
Do we really want the Kingdom to come?
What is the "Kingdom come?"
    Ah! The wonderful time
    The people in their misery long for:
    God obeyed, God in charge,
Righteousness,
Shalom! Peace! Goodwill!

Jesus said: "It is near, it is here.
I'll tell you what it's like," He said.
"I'll tell you what its people are like
Who rejoice while living it."

"This," He said to his following "is how
You will be living it,
You will be doing it, the Kingdom:
You will be humbly faithful;
You will be grieved by the sins of the people

But you will be gentle, courteous:
Longing for God's truth in all of life.
You will be merciful and kind.
You will build peace with the stable strength of LOVE,
The LOVE that crumbles every barrier.

Continued

Jesus said to His companions:
"You are to season all the earth
And to gleam across the gloom of the land."
You, who call yourselves Christians,
Who claim to be His disciples!

Will it happen today,
The Kingdom come,
His Will be done?

On Treasure and Trust
(Matthew 06:19-34; Luke 12:22-34)

We did not create ourselves
>   Nor form the force by which we live,
>   By which we strive,
>   By which we work for daily bread.

God gave the energy we put to work
That we might live and, living,
Provide for our own
And for those beyond our borders.

The manna grows stale the second day.
The unshared harvest rots
The money rusts or thieves may steal.

Do we, are we then also robbers of the poor
If we use God-given strength and the store that He supplies
To feed none but ourselves
And save abundance for our future ease
And pile up profits and store our accumulated toys?

Lord, teach us how to trust.
>   We hide behind the walls that shut us off
>   From those who sink in weakness,
>   In weariness, or starve.
We fear the phantom of want. And
"Who will care" we ask, "if not we for ourselves?"

Continued

Teach us to trust
Teach us to share thy bounty
Trusting love, and confident in faith.

Just think: If God be providence,
Perhaps He made us that we might be,
In His image, providers,
Creating, out of chaos, for our fellow-creatures.
Life, a living.

What then, if this be so
And we use our minds and might
To our advantage, disadvantaging the victims of our wealth,
Do we not, then, work against God and His intent for good?

Judge Not?
(Matthew 07:1-5, 10:24-25, Luke 06:41-42)

When we live under the Rule of God

We accept the norm God sets.
His righteousness.
Dependably, mercifully, He is just.
He is our criterion
By which we judge our thoughts and acts,
And the ways society takes
And the conduct and standards of others.

We are not God, all-seeing.
    Our human eyesight is not clear
And sometimes we adhere to patterns not God-given.
Lord, make us humble!
O, Holy Light, guide us
    That we not stumble.

So, with the Spirit's guidance, we will judge
    The right from wrong.
"Love righteousness and hate wickedness"
(So will we be anointed with the oil of gladness*)
And love, as God loves us, each other,
And faithfully do right by others, whoever they be
As God, in covenant forgiving,
Does right by us.

For in the kingdom we are taught
To condone no evil and yet
Not to condemn, as only God will do,
The evildoer lest we ourselves,
    If unrepentant, be condemned.

*Psalm 45:7

The Way
(Matthew 07:13-20)

What if we are
    What we would not wish to be:
Dull of understanding, blind to beauty,
    Deaf to the call of goodness
Unworthy of wisdom and wonder,
    Scuffing them under?

We can rise
    To Holy enterprise,
Reach for the stars,
    Climb over bars
Of mean and petty passions,
    Speak up and ask
Of God, the all-provider,
    And find what comes with eager searching
And open doors we always thought shut tight.
And share the glory from our gleaning
Give the goodness, glow the gladness.

The crowds cram through the easy ways
(Meandering masses seeking no salvation),
Luxuriate in what decays
    Spendthrift, careless, thoughtless days,
Frolic through some current fad
And fade and founder till life is lost.
How easy, oh, how sad! Lost!

The narrow gate, the total consecration!
Hard going? Rugged? Rough?
Giving – Not given to getting,
Going – Not liking to loiter,
Toughened by the effort,
Upward, onward, forward,
God-led and God-strengthened,
We tread the high and Holy places*   *Habakkuk 03:19
The way of love, the way of faith.

Call to Arms
(Matthew 08:19-22; Mark 01:12-20)

Our jobs—Our choice—Our livelihood
Hoping for a better world.
God calls—Do we respond?—Immediately?
Leave all. Tomorrow is here.
Jesus leads. Dare we follow?
Regardless of the ambient culture.
Standards, pressures, circumstance,
Live the better world, no waiting,
No compromise and no postponement.
One allegiance: God's rule.
Jesus' way.

Jesus and the Disciples, Apostles
(Matthew 11:28-30; Luke 06:12-13)

He talked it over with God, Father.

He spent all night in prayer;
Then He called them, and He chose them,
Just local folk, unstarred and untitled
And He talked to them
About the rule of God, the meaning
Of the realm of goodwill.
Then He showed them its loving-kindness.
Healing, helping the unwanted, lonely, outcasts,
Sinners, the untamed, the blemished and deranged,
Drawing them into fellowship.

But the Holy ones, they scorned Him
And the righteous ones, they spurned Him.

Then He talked it over with God, Father
Thankful that, though hidden from the wise and the learned.
From the teachers of the law, the proud mentors,
The way of the Lord
Was understood by the simple.

These He cared for, these He invited,
These who were burdened and weary, afflicted, neglected.
"Come to me," He said; "enter the Kingdom."
Drop your burdens, leave off worries and vain wishes.
The yoke of pure faith fits you better.
Learn of me, I am humble and gentle.

> "He who finds his life will lose it.
> He who loses life for my sake finds it."

> This is the true resurrection.

He Told Them Stories
(Matthew 13:10-15)

He told them stories,
Brief, pointed, from the common experience,
    And sometimes with a subtle twist.
They liked the stories, leaned forward to hear.
But did they hear,
That is, did they understand, take to themselves?
Did these stories make a brimming difference in the way they lived and
    What they lived for?

These were illustrations, that is what He said:
Illustrations of God's kingdom,
Of the great new day of the Lord,
The wonder day.

Did the people get the point?

Do we?
The kingdom of God
    About what will happen.
Has it happened?
Two thousand years have passed.
What happened?
Maybe they—we, too,—missed the point.
God ruling in human life.
No, not about a glorious day to come, sweet bye and bye
(We yearn for such a day).
Not a golden era passed and missed.
(Alas, we lost that day).
But now. What happens now
In us, by us, through us?
God's way, God's sway.

Oh, God! Lord of love in life,
So let it be! "Thy kingdom come!"

Transfiguration
(Matthew 17:1-8, 14-18)

Can we ascend the hill of aspiration?
Can we see with eyes of faith?
Can we come down again and deal compassion
In the vale
    And show a vision's brightness
        In the darkness?

Are we with Jesus and the saints on the mountain top?
Are we without Jesus with the crowds in the valley?
To follow Jesus to the mountain
    Is to understand who He is.
To go with Jesus in the valley
Is to do what He does.

Forgive
(Matthew 18:21-35)

The substance of the Gospel is "Love:"
Whereby Jesus is called "The Christ:"
Divine love in human demonstration,
Experienced in all forgiven,
Expression in full forgiving.

"How many times? Even to seven?
    Shall we count them? Say, "There's a limit!"

"Till seventy times seven!"
Then forgiveness is not a duty.
Nor a short sentiment or emotion.
It is habit divinely instilled.
    The character of wholly living,
    The charter of heaven,
        The forgiven, forgiving.

Forgiveness is the Gospel experienced.
Forgiveness: The Gospel expressed.
Forgiveness is love's definition,
Revitalizing God's creature.
The restoration of fellowship offered,
The true renewal of being.

Never Say the Day Was Wasted
(Matthew 19:30-20:16)

Never say the day was wasted
Or the life misspent.
The past is past.
What was is now forsaken.
The Master calls again.
"Come, your help is needed.
Put on your apron.
Get to work.
Soon it will be night.
You have a little while for labor
Do your very best.
I'll be beside you
And when the day is done,
Invite you to my rest."

(And so was, and so it shall be ever.
The first and last together,
Sharing the same reward.
All equal in the Master's care,
In the never-ending festival of love.)

The Wedding Feast
(Matthew 22:1-14)

INVITED—REJECTED

If the Lord invites me
    To the wedding feast of His Son
        What an honor!
        What a privilege!
            To be His guest   Among the rest
Nothing can hinder!

But yet, of course, **ME**!
    I have my interests and my concerns
        My own pleasures
        My priorities
            Then, if there's time   For a social climb
Insult and blunder!

UNINVITED—EXPECTED
I lived on the street
Unworthy to meet
Or sit at the feet
Of my Lord at His feast.

Yet His servants compelled
Me to come. I beheld
My Lord where He held
His Son's wedding feast.

Answer to the Herodians
(Matthew 22:15-22; Mark 12:13-17; Luke 20:20-26)

So Caesar claims it?
    Let him have it, so long as I keep my soul.
What God requires?
Let me give it, undivided, totally, whole!

Woe Is Me
(Matthew 23:1-36)

Look at the crowds,
    Watch the people.
How does God see them
    Under the steeple?
I have faith?
    Well, it doesn't appeal.
I have love?
    Well, it doesn't reveal.
I have the law?
    Well, it doesn't prevail.
I have respect?
    Well, the honor grows stale.

I wouldn't want
    Any "woes" on me!
Are my thoughts
    Where they ought to be?

I say one thing
    But God sees two:
The words I speak
    And the things I do.

Would my pride exclude
Common Folk from my tallies?
Do I guide them all
Into blind alleys?
Do I strain at a gnat
    And swallow a camel?
I praise prophets past
    But the present I trammel

What are my values?
What do I think?
I'm washed outside
But inside I stink.

God have mercy!
    The years I've passed
"A man of God"
    At the devil's task.

My house is forsaken,
    My innocence fled.
Who will awaken
    My hopes from the dead?

Jesus In Tears

(Matthew 23:37-39; Luke 13:34-39; Isaiah 05:1-7;
Jeremiah 12:7)

I

God loves you! God loves you?

God! The beginning! Creator of all! Everlasting!
Beyond whom none more ultimate!
Utter, perfect reality!
Justice requiring justice.
Righteousness relating, enabling, reconciling.
"God is love!"

Do we understand, now,
The communion times of Jesus with the Father?
He understood. He knew. He expressed
The sorrow born in Love. The suffering that yearns
For the fellowship of creature with Creator
In the miracle wonder of heaven immersed in earth.
Divine serenity infused in human crisis.
Eternity instilled in time.

II

God loves you! YOU God loves,
Chooses, blesses, provides for you.
Do you realize you make God suffer,
(Even God, like a parent in sorrow,
In grief for a child's desolation).

When you spurn the love that He offers,
And stray from the path that He proffers,
Transgress the terms of His goodness
In self-centered pride's provocation?
Mistreating, disdaining each other,
You thrust yourself out of His Eden,
In the sadness of Love, God is weeping.

Continued

III

Jesus stood on the hill near the city
In tears that were deeper than pity:
Invitation unanswered, uncared for,
God's people unpeopled in rancor.
A shaft of sunlight in shadows!
Or showers that wash through the meadows!
What sorrows are these, Lord, my Savior
At the falsehood in human behavior
Refusing the grace to which bidden
In greed that religion has hidden?

Ready for the Love-Feast?
(Matthew 25:1-13)

To be a part of the celebration!
    Chatter, laughter, anticipation.
We, the light-bearers for greeting the groom,
    To banish the shadows in the wedding room.

But weary with waiting, watching, and yawning.
    The sleepy night, passing, moves on toward dawning.
Why does he not come? Why does he tarry?
    The bride grows faint. Will they ever marry?

Ah, flickering wicks! The oil is fast burning!
    Haste to the market, fresh oil, quick returning!
Cheers! Hear the cry: "The bridegroom's at hand!"
    He really is coming! Strike up the band!

Quick, trim our lamps! Soak the wick! Hurry!... *But*
    The bridegroom goes in and the door is now shut!
We are late, but we're here. "Open up!" We implore.
    The wedding's in progress. No one opens the door.

"The bridegroom denies that he ever knew you.
    His friends are those with him, the ready, the true few."
Oh, why were we slothful, so wasteful of time?
Why were we unready for the love-feast sublime?

Keep oil in your lamp! Be alert! Be alive!
    Watch each hour for the Lord. He shall surely arrive!

The Great Investment
(Matthew 25:14-30)

What God has given me is not mine
    For I am His.
And what I have is only mine to do His will.

To reap from what I've sown His capital of love.
Investing all I own in the goodness He has shown,
To scatter, share, its blessing with the world.

God has entrusted me with life
That I may live for Him
And give for Him the riches of His grace,
That I may face each opportunity
Alert and true, responsibly
That I may bring to Him on that last day
The full abundance I have earned for Him.
And hear His glad approval and accept
The higher calling in His realm.

What God has given me is not mine
    For I am His,
And what I have is only mine to do His will.

Agony
(Matthew 25:31-46)

Who passed the sentence?
I?
I stand condemned.
But why?
    More agony than I could ever think for!

I was so much in a hurry, sir.
Doing my work.
I was jostled by the crowd, sir.
I did not shirk,
I just, well, never saw you there,
I was not tall.
I never knew you anywhere
To give my all.
I firmly stood by my belief,
My moral pride.
I could have given you relief
If I had tried.
I disdained, I must admit,
Hoi polloi;
I turned aside, I sought to quit
Those who annoy.

I saw you not, for my gaze was on my wanting.
I went *my* way, in isolation lost.
I swear I never saw nor heard you
In dark alleyways of human need and grieving.

    Alas, I spurned you, shut off.
    Shut off forever in the shadows!
    More agony than I could ever think for!

Joy
(Matthew 25:31-46)

Who passed the sentence?
I?
I stand commended!
But why?
    More joy than I dared ever wish for!

Of course I fed the hungry
For I can hunger, too,
Gave drink to those the thirsty
When throats were parched for moisture.
I would visit the sick as I have been
Or the lonely in prison where I could be,
The lost from homelands, I could welcome them home.
The poor in their tears
Human, like me, kindred in flesh,
I could weep with their grief,
I could suffer their pain.

These were you, my life's Master?
My Lord and my God, time's eternal Creator?
I never knew! But I loved you.

    And now—to inherit your kingdom forever?
Fellowship of compassion, no end of your caring!
    More joy than I dared ever wish for!

Judas of Kerioth
(Matthew 26:14-25; Mark 14:10-18; Luke 22:3-22)

What can we get out of God?
Will He not back up our goals?
Or is there a split twixt His purpose
And the patterns we set for our souls?

Perhaps we'll best profit our cause
Selling Him who now fails our desires,
Deserting this Jesus, stern Prophet,
Forsaking the fools He inspires.

Judas, what pure aspiration
Enflamed your once high-aiming breath?
You traded your dream for time's treasures
You trashed all your hopes by His death.

CHAPTER 2

BOOK OF MARK

Among the Many
(Mark 01:1-13; Matthew 03:13-4:1)

The news spread far and wide
    About the preacher in the desert,
    About the herald of the day of the Lord.
From far away they came and from nearby
To hear His words, in hope and fear
To wash away their sins, yet not
So much to escape the wrath of God
As to be ready for the Messiah who would come.

Among the many there came one
(But who would know Him?)
For baptism and the baptizer gasped.
"You! Not you by me, I need baptism by you!"
But this one who came, like all the others,
    Went down into the waters
And He saw, like a dove of pure beauty,
    A spirit of peace, perch on His head.
And He heard a voice no man could speak:
"This is my beloved Son in whom I am well pleased,
The semblance of my love."

Who could this be?
How would He do?
What would He say?

He came, He went away
Divinely present, humanly weak. He walked away,
Into the wilderness.

Dare We Follow?
(Mark 01:16-20; Luke 09:57-62)

They walked away from where they were.

They walked to where He was.
They left their nets, their source of food.
They came to Him, the source of Life.
They looked to Him and saw no more the glitter of their treasures
They listened to Him and heard no more the clatter of their pleasures.

    They who hesitate are lost!
    They who stop to count the cost!

    Abandonment of self with full intent!
    Attachment to their Lord whom God had sent!
    They quickly rose, leaving their nets.
    They followed Him without regrets.

Beatitude
(Mark 01:16-22)

Disciples!
Jesus called them. Were they committed?
   Did they understand?
God's realm!
Love's rule!
   A new era   A new way to live.
   Could they, would they, live it?

Disciples!
Jesus called us, are we committed?
      Do we understand?
God's realm!
Love's rule!
   A new era   A new way to live.
   Can we, do we, live it?

Not to gain wealth
   But *to live simply*—where God is ruling.
Not to win bounty
   But *in love sharing*—there is contentment.
Not seeking pleasure
   But *to bear others' burdens*—here is true gladness.
Not for applause;
   Just *Christ to follow*—Christ our reward.

Capernaum
(Mark 01:32-37)

In Nahum's town -

A long and wondrous evening!
Town folk would never forget.
Remember how they crowded 'round?
His words lighted up a bright new time,
Awoke their hopes, turned ashes into beauty. Go away.

"This," they thought, "our friends must hear,
Our sick, our sad, our strange-behaving neighbors."

All evening long they were bringing people to His side.
This Jesus surely all must see and all make well.

He looked with such compassion, remember?
He smiled on them and touched them.
Touched their sores, opened their eyes, their ears
They heard new things they'd never heard before.
He breathed a healing love.
They sparked alive with gleaming joy.

We, too?

All through that wondrous night…

    In the pre-dawn dark He left them
        Restored, renewed, reflecting the divine.

"Stay, Jesus, stay! Don't go away…!"

Where will we go to find Him?

Alone
(Mark 01:32-39)

Alone? With God.
The whole world in His heart.

Begin at home,
Capernaum, where faith holds strong.

Abroad
Through little Galilee
Wherever people of faith gather

The circles will grow wider.
All God's people!
Who can set limits?
    The neighbor, the friend, the kinfolk, the stranger, the enemy.

    Why, sir Jesus,
        Why did you pray? God's presence.
        What did you preach? God's rule.
        How did you heal? God's caring.
        Why drive out devils? God's power.
What moves you, Sir Jesus, that you so move others? Compassion.

Will your loving-kindness move us as well?
Among the multitude,
If you go, will we go with you?

After a long evening, healing the sick that were brought to Him
    And casting out devils,
They all went to their beds, Jesus too.
But Jesus rose from His bed well before day.
He went into a desert place to pray. What was His prayer?

First Peter, then other disciples—then a crowd of town folk found Jesus.
"Why did you leave us? Everyone is looking for you. Please stay!"
    Jesus went through Galilee teaching, healing.

The Galilean Prophet
(Mark 01:32-44; Luke 11:53-54)

Who is this kindly person walks among us,
Whose gentleness betrays a strength of being?

He does not fit our formula.
He follows not the paths we have staked out.
Does not fulfill our expectations.

He often stirs our pride to ego anger,
But never hurts a humble heart to tears.

There is an inner spirit moves Him
A breath from God breathes through Him,
A mighty mercy that controls Him
A force that heals, restores revives the true creation.

Do we understand Him?

Jesus' Family
(Mark 03:33-35)

When He swept His hand toward us
    And said, "These are my family," did He mean *we* are?
Or, perhaps, only when we do?
Do we go apart in the quiet, and commune, as He did
    In the vivid joy of our Father's presence?

What is this that vibrates among us when we gather in His company?
We walk beside, or a little behind, Him.
Do we see what He saw in every passing person:
    The sacred delight of God in all His creatures?
Do our hearts weep, as His did,
    When we see their bodies suffer,
Their minds and hearts self-tortured,
Their lives exploited,
Their being disdained, excluded?
Do we trust and thrust the power of love for healing in their lives?
Is this "The will of God:" To spend our lives for others?

Is this the mark of Jesus' Family?

Yet He Loved Them
(Mark 06:34)

Alone You stood
On the brow of the hill
Your heart was bleeding.

The multitude
Breathed of God's breath,
Yet never heeding.

You healed their wounds,
Cast out distress
And fed their needing.

They turned away
They spurned your words,
Your love impeding.

Who? Where? How?
(Mark 09:42; 11:22-23; Matthew 18:6-7; Luke 16:19-31)

Indifferent to the paupered poor outside our door.

Unconcerned for the youth enticed to shame and sin.

Unforgiving of offenders of our dignity and pride.

Jesus calls us to follow?
    Where do you go, Lord? Where do we find you?
Where Lazarus lies among the dogs,
Where children cry in unsheltered streets,
    And the weak pant for breath,
Where the unfit are tossed aside and punished,
    Unacquainted with grace.

Faith!—"Increase our faith, Lord!"
    For what?
That we may heal the sick of body, mind and heart,
That we may feed the hungry with our bread,
That we may share the burdens of the frail,
And take the hand of the stumbling child,
And widen our fellowship to include
    Society's failures, fumblers, to
        Give them hope, new life restored by love.

In the Synagogue at Nazareth
(Mark 06:1-6; Luke 04:16-30; Matthew 13:53-58)

Mostly the Nazarenes were poor, sequestered,
Shadowed by the proud Sepphoris,
Scorned and scoffed at, yet were they not
Abram's children, praised by prophets,
Blessed by God, the righteous people?
Disdain the worldly, scurvy Gentiles!

Jesus, local carpenter, known to all the town,
Reading the prophet Isaiah
About health, freedom, good days to come.
What will neighbor Jesus say?

He says fair words. "The time has come,"
He says. Gracious words! He could say more
To sweeten them to go His way, politically astute,
He could rouse their anger
At the oppressor Rome, press them to violence
Against the evil foe as many Zealots did.
But no!
The Godly heroes of His comments
Were the enemy, the heathen, alien.

God's justice—this He dares to say—
Rules equally over all because
God's mercy has no favorites
But is dispensed most richly on the sick,
The disabled, the despised
Who appeal to His compassion.

So saying, Jesus led on the prophet's course,
The pattern for all time   That
Spokesmen for peace, for universal love
For healing action are not acceptable
To pride, to the violence of power.
So the Nazarenes, real religious folk,
Rejected Him.

Faith slipped through the threatening crowd,
No miracle could be done.

The Rule of Love
(Mark 10:1-16)

Rules are when the faith fades low
And life is run by regulations.

Human rules—the flesh is weak—
Allowance made for fluctuations.

But yet there is a Rule that rules
The soul committed in relations:

The rule of Love that supersedes
All social codes that strap the nations,

Breaches barriers, bridges, moats,
Reconciles from alienations,

Love that weaves a holy bond
Holding sacred marriage vows,
Forbears, forgives, freely to share
Self with self, unmeasured care.

Love that lifts a child to bless,
Affection, guardian from distress:
The child, whose trust and open heart
Reflect God's kingdom's holy art.

The Rich Ruler
(Mark 10:17-31)

The chance came.
The opportunity occurred.
The vision appeared.
Its glory I glimpsed.
With hope I desired it.
How can I reach it, the ultimate,
    Life of the ages, the everlasting?

There is *one* who must know,
    Who appears like its realness.
Ask: "What can I do to inherit eternal life?"

"Keep the law of life! Do the right, refrain from wrong."

"Oh, I do! I do! What more?
How can I delve into the depth?
    Capture the full extent of life beyond life?"

For a moment I am bathed in the smile of God,
    A glow of love around me.
"One thing you lack.
    One thing left 'tween you and the realm of God.
Leave all you have,
    The trappings of time,
        The weights of world-weavings,
            The wants and the wastings

Continued

And freely give, share, give!
Food for the famished,
    Joy for the cheerless.
        Succor for the suffering,
            Sunlight in the shadows,
                Beauty for the blemished.
And come, join with us, the fellowship of giving."

Ah! "Eternal life!" "Kingdom of God!"
Yes?   No?
Leave all! For all! All?
The sunlight is shaded, its glory eclipsed.
    The vision has faded
Opportunity vanished.   The chance is gone.

Sacrifice of the Servant
(Mark 11-12)

We had been with Him many months.

Walking with Him, talking with Him, eating with Him and resting nights
    Beside the road as He spent the hours in prayer.
Conversation He would have with God-
    As a son with his father,
    As a child with his mother;
Contemplation He would have in the silence
    A communing with God
    As a soul with its source.

We were with Him
    But we did not know Him.
We saw His deeds of compassion
But did not see the seer of human suffering
We heard His words of God's kingdom
    But did not hear the hearer of human sorrow.

That week (we call 'Holy') the heavens opened a window to the world.

    First day: With the throng He entered the city in triumph.
        They were shouting "Hosanna!"
Then why did He leave in silence, going so meekly to the village?

    Second day: With authority He cleansed the temple.
        He was saying: "My Father's house!"
Then why did He leave in the dusk-light, going soft to the hillside?

    Third day: With reason and stories He taught God's rule for living.
        And He counseled His companions.
    So why did men seek to destroy Him, plotting secretly murder?

Continued

Fourth day: We cannot help but wonder,
  What would happen on Wednesday?
    We disciples waiting…the hours fleeting
      And beside us…yet apart
        Jesus reporting to the Father,
          Resting in His grace,
            Receiving His commands,
              Breathing in the sacred breath,
            Eternity in time.
  How will we face tomorrow?

He Comes
(Mark 11:1-10; Matthew 31:1-9; Luke 19:28-38; John 12:12-15)

"**J**esus of Nazareth?"

Oh, yes, the "prophet of Galilee"!
The crowds, wherever He goes, follow Him
Who heals their sick, casting out demons,
Restores sight and hearing with loving compassion.
He tells stories. They listen,
A practical guide to good-willing.
Even, they say, He forgives sinners, feeds the hungry…
    Could *this* be the longed-for "Messiah"
    Heir to David's throne, the King of the Jews?

Coming! To restore Israel's glory.
The Lord's Day is here!
    The time of reckoning, the age of God's Realm.
Ah, He comes! He is coming!
For this day we were waiting.
In this hope we were living.
See! The King of creation!
Triumphant. Victorious.
    Humble, riding on a donkey.
        A colt, the foal of a donkey.
He comes!
Speaking peace to the nations,
Holy rule for all people.
    HOSANNA!
    Let us gather to praise Him.
    Let us join His disciples.
    Let us never be faithless,
    Like the fickle who fail Him,
    Let us crown Him! *Our Master.*
        Right now and forever!

Authority
(Mark 11:27-33; Matthew 21:23-27; Luke 20:1-8)

What is His authority?
Who gave to Him the right
    To teach, to care, forgive,
        To save, and heal?

He is the authority.
And He gives to us the right
    (And if we will accept it)
    To care, to heal, and bless.
    To share the word that saves.

    Forgiving love is its own authority
    Which none can ration or withhold.
    It is the divinely ultimate,
    Creation's greatest power.

On the Way to Jerusalem
(Mark 10:32-52; Luke 19:1-10)

On the road.

The Zebedees, disciples:
We believe in you, Lord.
   In you is our hope,
A goodness that draws us;
   A greatness amazing...
We follow you, Lord, but
As God's one anointed
   You are destined for glory.

   All this talk about suffering sounds like surrender!
   No, it does not suit our plan for you.
   The vigor, the power, the sovereignty:
   That is your future
      To which we are linked.

And so, we ask a favor.
Please fulfill our ambitions,
Your companions in splendor
Ranking beside you, reflecting your luster.

   "Drink the cup you will drink of?"
   "Immersed in your baptism?"
   Yes, though not understanding,
   Whatever—We are able—
   Just so we are with you.
      Your strength we will live by,
      Your love we will cling to.

Continued

In Jericho.
Persistent Bartimaeus, blind beggar:
Blind like Bartimaeus, "Jesus, let me see!"
Nothing will deter me, "Son of David, I must see!"
Thou wilt surely heal me. "Lord I must, will, see."
Wonder! Sight restored! "Christ, I will follow thee!"

Persistent Zacchaeus, extortioner:
Sinner, like Zacchaeus, "Jesus I must see!"
Little, low of stature, "I will climb a tree."
Insistent, I must see thee! "Thou wilt call to me."
Enter, Christ, my dwelling. "I will give for thee."

Live to God
(Mark 12:18-27; Matthew 22:23-33; Luke 20:27-40)

PHARISEES:
We thought we were God's people.
But we were trampled on and scorned.
Surely, there must be vindication.
Surely God will do right by us
Since we are His and praise Him
(Yet there is no praise or promise in the grave)
Ah! We will rise from the grave, that should do it!
-But only, of course, if we are righteous
Having kept the laws of God!
Then shall the wicked be punished.
God will avenge Himself and us!

SADDUCEES:
Fools!
Keep the Laws, live well
For all must die. There's no assurance otherwise in Sacred Writ.
Use the NOW cleverly for your best.
For nothing lasts and all feasts end.

JESUS:
You speak of the Living God!
God is God of the living, not of the dead.
Why do you minimize the Living God to less than your limited minds?
Why do you materialize the Living God to existence and no more?

Death, a step in God's creation,
Cuts existence short, it stops the breathing.
To resurrect the dead to exist again
A few more days or years does not deny
The ending of time's Genesis.

But they who, existing, live to God,
Inspired by His Holy breath,
Enlivened with His purpose and His will,
Enveloped in the was and is and shall forever be,
Encompassed by His love eternally.

How Should We Live?
(Mark 12:28-31)

How should we live?

Remember, primary reality of all creation is God, the creator.

He made us...why?
> He made us, in love, to be what truly we can be!

He chose us...why?
> He chose us, in love, to be most surely His children!

He showed us...why?
> He showed us, in love, how purely we may live.

He loves us...why?
> He loves us that we rightfully may love Him.

How?
> With our hearts entirely, our total, moral consciousness;
> With our souls entirely, our total adoration;
> With our minds entirely, our total intellect and thought;
> With our strength entirely, our total force and being;
>> With all that we are.

This is no rule or regulation.
It is closeness to the heavenly Father;
It is nearness to His will.

> And what then does this mean?
> That all people, all the creator's human creatures,

Are our neighbors, all to love
> As we love ourselves.
> All to serve and care for
> With the love by which God loves.

Thus should we live.

For Pharisees and Scribes, and Rulers and All of Them and Us
(Mark 12:37-40; Matthew 23:1-36; Luke 20:45-47)

Oh Lord God, root out
>   From me, from us, from those who lead
>   And dominate, their little while, our times,
>   Expressions of faith that fail in fact and act
>   To match or meet the righteousness of truth,

That cover up, in deed, the underlying sin:
>   Self-seeking pride, deception, and disdain
>   For the very folk they do pretend to save,

The prudish pieties that screen the hidden avarice and greed,
>   Wanton destructions in the earth,
>   Violence vaunted as valor protecting the law
>   While devouring widows and the poor,
>   And burdening their children and the weak.

Oh, save us yet
>   From all who parade their schemes
>   In the guise of the gospel, who,

In the name of good transgress against God's grace
And who, in the framework of religion
>   Rack up rules that wreck rather than build
>   And gild their witless wastings of our wealth
>   The beauties of life thy love has wrought.

The Widow's Mite
(Mark 12:41-44; Luke 21:1-4)

I thought I saw the saints about God's throne.

Though poor and humble and of shabby dress
Their faces bore a radiance all their own,
A sweet and caring kindness no distress
Could efface.

They were the souls who spent their lives each day
And all they were and all that they possessed
Not to accumulate and keep but give away
And through their poverty the earth was blessed.
A holy grace!

The House of God
(Mark 13:1-4; Matthew 24:1-3; Luke 21:5-7)

Do we build our temples, stone by stone

As grand memorials to our faith,
Yet let our zeal be ever prone
To pride provoking hate?

For the house of God, the Spirit's home,
Constructed is by praise and prayer.
Its turrets and its towers and dome
Are the love and hope we share.

Rejoice
(Mark 13:5-37; Matthew 24:4-36; Luke 21:8-36)

"I will create new heavens and a new Earth…be glad and rejoice forever…" Isaiah 65:17-18

The world is weary with its worries,
    With its wickedness and woes,
With its sufferings and sorrows,
    With oppressions from God's foes.

Thou Eternal One, Creator,
    Wipe away this age of strife,
Send us succor, give us courage
    For a new and better life.

A new earth and a new heaven.
    Speak, Lord, that, hearing thy voice
We thy people, loved, forgiven,
    All, forever, will rejoice.

Troubled Yet Steadfast
(Mark 13:9-13; Mathew 24:9-14; Luke 21:12-19)

To Christ we have sworn our allegiance!
Why, then, this persecution?
Must we be loyal to His compassion
When tormenters tear our bodies
And bare our souls before vindictive judgment?

To Christ we now speak out our witness.
No fear can fret or afright us,
No storm sweep aside His sure presence.
No sound can drown out His message.

But, alas, conflicts rage all around us.
Our people turn sternly against us.
They scoff and they scorn, they betray us
Yet, our Lord will never forsake us.

Our Master says, "Do not be anxious!
My voice will speak my Word through you.
Trust! I will always be with you,
My Spirit be standing beside you,
Calm courage in stress I will give you."

From Christ we'll not panic or scatter,
We will bravely endure, never matter!
God's love is steadfast and faithful
Our hope, everlasting sustainer.

This the disciples' true calling:
To Christ we have sworn our allegiance,
His joy we will share with all people.
    Till His story all mankind confesses,
        Till His glory the wide world professes
            Till all, reconciled in kindness,
                Are expressions of God's lasting goodness.

Gethsemane

(Mark 14:32-42; Matthew 26:36-46; Luke 22:38-46)

Ah, but did you ever agonize so seriously
–Refusing to rest,
–Refusing to run,
–Struggling with death,
–Striving with life,
Until the sweat bathed your brow?
    And the blood oozed from your flesh?

Thus prayed our Lord.
    To do God's will
        When, in His earnest devotion
            His work seemed not done
            Nor God's kingdom won.
But losing Himself completely
        In the flow of fervent Love.

Only then, only then, came the angel
        To fortify His faith
Only now, only now, could He rise
        In triumph to see God's face.

The Finish
(Mark 15:24-33; Matthew 27:39-49, 55-56; John 19:25-30)

There were soldiers with their spears.
There were rulers with their sneers.
There were women with their tears.
Why did He die?

They taught laws all should obey.
They told rules, a holy way.
They warned off who go astray.
Why did they lie?

Love hangs bleeding on a tree.
Love brought hope and made us free.
Love gave all that we may be.
Why pass Love by?

Darkness creeps across the earth.
Wisdom wonders at its worth.
Sadness seeks a second birth.
The heavens sigh.

Is done! The great transaction's done.
Finished! His task. The victory's won.
The Father's will lives through the Son.
The Cross is high!

Mary Magdalene
(Mark 16:1,9; Matthew 28:1; Luke 24:10-12; John 20:1-18)

Oh! Mary Magdalene, of seven devils cleansed,
Pure, in holy Love, in dedication's blend,
You will not, will not, let Him go.
At the cross, yes, at the very tomb
In the garden, "Where have they laid Him?
That even there I may go and find Him!"

"Go, tell and ask the disciples:
They have taken away my Lord. Where will I find Him?"

Two go. They come to see the tomb is vacant.
Wondering, they go home. The others hide themselves.

Back to the garden, Mary, weeping.
"What, woman, why the sorrow?"
"Gardener? Sir, tell me where my Master lies?
There will I mind Him."

    You will not let Him go!

Mary Magdalene, you will not go from Him.
Through life, through death, to the very end His breath
Through you will breathe.
For you, your faith, that you believe;
You cling to Him and so, 'tis we,
The millions through millennia can be
Expressions of eternity, a victory of meaning, mercy.

O Mary Magdalene, of seven devils cleansed,
Pure, in holy Love, in dedication's blend,
You will not, will not, let Him go!
You will not go from Him. Nor yet shall we.
Go tell His disciples: "He lives! He Lives!"
And we, self crucified with Him:
In Him, by Him, "we too shall live!"

CHAPTER 3

BOOK OF LUKE

Our Last, But Lasting Message

(Luke 02:25-38)

We waited by the temple door, Anna and I,
Surely we could wait no more where the high priest stood,
Assured authority in blue
Who knew
No Christ could come without His signature and crest.

Yet we had blessed
The little one in threadbare blanket
Borne and born by a maid simple and sweet
Who dared not even bow at the high priest's feet.

"Simeon," Anna had said, "We've waited. He has come.
He always will be coming to those who wait."
"They will see Him and be blessed," I said.

We know the time has come for us to go.
We leave a prayer, an ardent wish, a plea
That passers-by may see,
When He is grown,
Made out of stubble and of clay a throne,
Served by the suffering, the ill
Outcast from the synagogue, the church,
Left to fend for themselves, left in the lurch.
Now comrade—servants of the Prince Shalom.

That they may hear compassion's healing
And behold
God's temple never made of currency and gold
But built with strong gentleness,
Pillared with Love on plinths of kindliness
Buttressed with pietistic faith,
A house where profane vengeance has no home,
Nor violence nor merchandise for gain.

God hails Him.
God bless you.
We must go.

The Word and the Touch
(Luke 05:12-16; Matthew 08:1-4; Mark 01:40-45)

Can we identify with the leper,
    Unclean, unclaimed, unacceptable,
Diseased, dirty, despised,
    Yet determined to be healed, made whole?
He charged into the crowd, which was against the rules.
He boldly approached this Jesus and cried,
"You can cleanse me if you want to."
He had faith.
Jesus replied, "I want to," and he touched Him,
Jesus defied the law that said,
"The man is cursed by God and cannot be cured."
Jesus disregarded the code that said,
"If you touch him you will be defiled with his defilement."

Jesus spoke the **WORD** that was above the law.
Jesus touched him with love and he was healed.

Kingdom Disciples
(Luke 06:12-16, 9:1-6)

The kingdom of God!—of *God*, you say?
The rule, the plan, the way of the eternal?

To present it? Represent it? Teach it to the world?
You'll need men of mettle,
Well educated,
    Highly respected,
        Qualified leaders,
            Saints perfected.
Right?

Whom does He choose, the Lord of life?
    Whom will He send?
Four fishermen!
    Two unskilled villagers!
        A mean collector of taxes!
            And a man unsure, and doubting!
And a "shorty James" and a "Tad". Who were they?
    And a guerilla type and a man who'll turn a traitor.

To these poor twelve He gave authority
    And sent them into the world. They went.
(He might even choose you, enable you, send you.
        Even you! Or me!
        Will we do as He did?)

What is the kingdom of God? Can we show it?
    Can we live it?

Christ's disciples.
God's children.

Cost and Courage
(Luke 09:1-6, 10, 22-26, 12:32-34)

The disciples sang this song in heart,
(Yet sometimes they forgot)

"We would go with you, sir Jesus.
We were not ready quite for this, however.
Crashing into the world,
Clashing crises all around."

"Fear not!" You said. "We do not fear
    Except to be separated, sir, far from you."

"We would be with you, in the eye of the storm,
The onrush of unimpeded love."

Long after we and our times are past,
May the passion of Christ pervade.

Transfiguration
(Luke 9:28-42)

Can we ascend the hill of aspiration?
Can we see with eyes of faith?
Can we come down again and deal compassion
In the vale
    And show a vision's brightness
        In the darkness?

Are we with Jesus and the saints on the mountain top?
Are we without Jesus with the crowds in the valley?
To follow Jesus to the mountain is to understand who He is.
To go with Jesus to the valley is to do with Him what He does.
Peace and beauty on the celestial hill.
Pressed with duty in the smelly, sordid crowd.

The Seventy
(Luke 10:1-9, 16-17)

In such a short time
>   You showed us;
In such a short time
>   You sent us
>   To speak with your accents,
>   To act as your presence,
>   To draw all the people
>   From stupor to steeple.
>   From darkness to dawn light,
>   From guilthood to God—Might
To God's righteousness which You spelt in redemption
To God's kingdom which you spoke in compassion.

By your strength we were enabled
To heal the disabled,
To relieve from pain and sorrow
With the hope of God's tomorrow
We proclaimed as your prophets
The realm You have promised.

But yet we were helpless
And still we were hopeless
Except by your power
By your glory each hour.
The demons we vanquished
And delivered the anguished
By the sword of your spirit,
The word of your merit.

Loving-Kindness
(Luke 10:27; Matthew 22:37-40; Mark 12:29-31)

There was another word the ancient Hebrew used for love.

The kind of feeling that stirs the heart with caring for someone
And when they used it when aware of God
It became the major force of faith and of a firm society.
This is how they reasoned:

God, the one who always was, is, will be. Ruler almighty.
The one who caused, causes, will cause, creator.
Who chose a people He created,
Who loved them, loves them still, who gives life meaning…
(Why do you ignore Him, or try to use Him for your convenience?)
Who taught you how to live, to love, your judge
("Love your neighbor as you love yourself.")
You feel for the one you love; your neighbor. Your fellow creature.
Be kind, friendly, helpful. For your neighbor belongs to your company.
So do the strangers, make them at home.
Hold them dear, clasp them, seek them out, be faithful
As God sought you out and sticks by you.

Return, exchange that love, for you it will be life.
Love God with all your heart, soul, strength
Seek Him, to be near Him, cleave to Him.
Give Him your total love.
Yes, love God intensely with all the energy you have

This love (Ahabh) is the web of being.

Teach Us to Pray
(Luke 11:1-4; Matthew 6:9-13)

"**F**ather!"

O God, now I may call thee "Father"
God! Judge and ruler over all your creation!
"Father" to Jesus who conversed with you
    Long nights in wilderness or on the mountainside,
    Or in the early dawn.
    Or at table with disciples.
        And in lonely agony of garden and cross!

"Our Father"
We—together in you, with you—
We pray to you, our Father.
    May your name be sacred on our lips, holy awe and wonder!
    May your rule be hallowed in our lives,
Your will for which we live.
We trust in you, our Father.
    You provide our sustenance every single day.
        We need not fear, nor worry
    You forgive us for our sins,
        Revive us by your mercy,
            Rekindle us with love,
        Remake us in your image, ready to forgive,
            Canceling each other's debts,
            Restoring us to fellowship
                With you, with one another.
We trust in you, our Father.
    To keep our feet from stumbling on trash we trample over,
    To guard us from perdition our faults would drive us to
    And from the isolation our selfness centers in.

We are our Father's children.
We are our Lord's disciples.

Help Us Pray
(Luke 11:1)

Lord, help us pray!
We need not say
What may approve itself to a listening ear,
But only that which Thy Spirit alone may hear.
For there is little time that's left,
The only while is yet.
Thou art within that yet.
Thee alone, O Lord,
And each alone with Thee
And the holy company.
Let Thy Holy Water pour,
The Holy Spirit pour,
Splash the soul, splash the whole
Of the moments that linger at the bowl
Of the cistern.

Father
(Luke 11:2; John 20:17)

Old Testament Religion never called God "father"

    Although it did use "father" as a metaphor
"as a father pities his children…"
but the intimacy of father in the home was never present.
There was to be—as there continues to be—the danger of sentimentalized intimacy.

The word Ahabh (aw-habh) did, however,
Leave the door openable between God and man.
Jesus opened that door.
He called God "Father" and "my Father" and,
"my Father and your Father."
Especially in the "Lord's Prayer"!
"Teach us to pray," His disciples said to Jesus.
    He taught them:
        "Our Father…" ***"OUR FATHER!"***
    What could be closer, or more confidentially dear than that?
But there is a qualification very important to remember:
"Our Father *in heaven*."
There is a distance: God in Heaven, we on earth.
        God infinite, unlimited, eternal,
            We, finite, limited, transient.
And yet, here is the incarnation that Paul understood so well:
    God, the Father, adopts us as His children.
    Invites us into His House,
    His infinity engulfing our finity,
    His limitlessness surrounding our limitations,
    His Eternity embracing our stroke of time,
    His omnipotence enabling our potential.

...and speaking of Beelzebub
(Luke 11:14-26; Matthew 09:32-34)

Clean up your house

And leave it bare?
While you're away
May enter there
An unclean spirit.
So beware!

The soul not filled
With love and grace
Leaves room for self
In empty space
And self grows stale,
Stagnates the place.

What Is Religion?
(Luke 11:14-12:4)

Do we need miracles to prove Jesus?

Is what we think to be light really darkness?
    May what we call good really be bad?
Is our religion Pharisaic?
Weren't the Pharisees good people, earnest about moral law?
Is the religion we practice worth living? Worth dying for?

Signs
(Luke 11:29-36)

"Give us a sign," they said.
"So then we can be sure…
A wonderment, you know, a super sapient glow,
A testimony from the skies,
    A sudden thunder's loud surprise."
"Then we'll know."

They fashion tales to satisfy their dreams.
They formulate their creeds: synthetic schemes
Of absolutes, conceited certitudes
And then they say, "We are the wise who see!
We are secure. We have a framework that excludes
The doubting multitudes who disagree."

He said: "You hypocrites! You're blind.
Saying you see, you lead others of your kind.
And when you fall into the wayside ditch
How will you know the way or what is which?"

Lord, sometimes it is dark. No path is clear.
No magic miracle; no flashing star to steer
Our course, and no neat code to guide.
We cling to YOU! To You and none beside.

Your message and Your presence now appear.

Clean
(Luke 11:37-41; Matthew 23:25-26)

Proper behavior,
In the words of our Savior,
Is cleaning the inside.
Set no store on the outside.

The sign of the Kingdom
Is true trust and wisdom.
Not law-keeping blindness,
But goodness and kindness.

The Moral Zealots
(Luke 11:42-52; Matthew 23:13-37)

The Pharisees (the pure ones) were godly men.
>   Were they not?

The Scribes (the doctors of the law) were wise men.
>   Were they not?

<u>They</u> thought so.
The people (the common folk) supposed they were.
God (the righteous one) gave them laws.
>   Did He not?

And He requires that His people obey the laws.
>   Does He not?

These leaders were so earnest
>   To understand,
>> To explain,

To observe,
>   The moral code in minute detail.

This would please God!
This would ensure that His anointed one would come!
And reward and save His people, the law-keepers.

Why then did this radical reformer from Nazareth
Come and condemn them?

In detailing God's rules they neglected God's rule.
In enforcing regulations they oppressed the poor,
>   Cast out the weak.

Their pretentious pride cloaked injustice.
Their passion for prestige smothered mercy.
Their rigid religion substituted true faith.
But truly they *were* religious men.

Would we be religious?
Vaunt morality?
Defend the faith?
Witness to it?
Win gentiles?
The way they did, the Pharisees, the Scribes?

Beware the Leaven of the Pharisees
(Luke 12:1)

God, the Father, was His center of life
    Hence His compassion for people.
The Law of God was their center for life
    Hence their perfection their passion.
If God's true will can be spelt out in rules
    We achieve it through strict regulations.
If God's true will is effected in Love
    His Spirit alone will express it.

What is the leaven that permeates us?
Perhaps, as for Pharisees, it's Religion.
Perhaps, like Herodians; worldly wisdom.
Perhaps, like the Sadducees, it's our status.
Or maybe, as for pagans, it's our pleasure
That impels our life-styles and our purpose.

Oh, God, our Father in Heaven,
We surrender our souls to Thy leading,
Breathe Thou Thy Spirit all through us,
That not we, but be Thou, our full action.

Contrasts - Discipleship vs
(Characteristics of discipleship according to Luke 12:4-48)

1) Courage vs Fear
2) Commitment to Christ vs Self-preservation
3) The kingdom of God vs The passing world
4) Self-giving vs Covetousness
5) Trust vs Anxiety
6) God at the center vs Self at the center
7) Value and good measured by divine will
    vs The wealth and power of false "security."

The Company of Disciples
(Luke 12:4-12; Matthew 10:28-33)

Did you call us to be in your company?

Did we respond and come?
Or did we ask to join you?
Did you weigh, accept, our pledge?

With a company command:
Bold witness, dexterous expression
Of Your love. Fearless,
Loyal, unhesitating,
Untrammeled with time's ordinary cares.

Our hope in God when joy anticipates His will.
Jubilantly free, we wait, alert,
Eager to exert our faith
Responsibly in you,
Your company. With You.

God Loves Them
(Luke 13:34-35, 19:41; Matthew 23:37-39; John 12:27)

Alone, Jesus stood, on the brow of the hill,
Weeping over Jerusalem.
"How often would I gather your children,
As a hen gathers her brood under her wings,
But you were not willing."

He yearned, His heart burning
With deep love for their turning.
He implored them, to restore them
To life's truth, all discerning.

He announced God's new kingdom,
The desire of all ages,
He invited their coming
And explained true commitment.

They ate of His bread;
They were glad for His healing,
They heard all His stories,
But neglected His teaching.

Love's cost: self-surrender,
Was too dear for their paying.
Christ's way, full compassion,
Too demanding to follow.

Alone, our Lord Jesus.
Draw us into your heartache.
We would share your soul longing
For the world, all earth's people.

What's Your Hurry?
(Luke 13:41-56, 17:20-37)

What's your hurry, Lord?
You just now came among us.
All we ask is comfort,
Peace for the passing moment.

No preachment to disturb us!
No call for stern obedience!
You do the kindly service.
We'll be your nice, good people.

What's your hurry, Lord?
You call us to repentance!
"Turn around and follow"
Where paths of mercy lead us.

No half-way measures matter!
To follow you or scatter.
No sentimental notion
But absolute devotion.

Time ticks towards life's last hour!
The wind of passion's power
Will slam the door forever.
Be reconciled…or never!

Your urgent call, heart-rending,
"God's kingdom's not an ending.
'Tis now, each moment spending.
Love—To every soul extending."

This is our hurry, Lord.
We wait not for tomorrow.
Love's deep compassion pressing.
Joy penetrates earth's sorrow.

The Great Invitation
(Luke 14:15-35)

We enter His kingdom by our Lord's invitation.

We do not achieve it by our good deeds.
The kingdom's no hobby performed when we please
No cushiony comfort, no soft pleasant breeze.

We hardly would have thought, and seldom think,
Eternity's divine and human link,
God's greatest gift: ability to give,
A dominating love by which to live.
God's kingdom's glory is His spirit's control,
A holy motivation, a soul's single goal,
A heavenly impulse in plans and in acts
That saturates relationships and pacts.
A flavor in the daily tasks we do,
A prayer approach to everyone, caring, true.
A savor in the work routinely done.
A faith by which hope's victory is won.

An atmosphere of kindness,
Environment of gladness,
An ambience of goodness,
Joy that prevails in sadness.

The kingdom of God is responsibility to God.
The kingdom of God is responsibility to life.
Responsibility to friend, stranger, and foe.
Responsibility wherever we are to go.

God's kingdom comes to us like a chariot of fire.
The offer is at hand, if we aspire,
If we repent, turn 'round, to walk love's way,
The invitation stands: the cross, the Christ, today.

God's Love for the Sinner
(Luke 15)

How can it be?
Such perfection of humanity.
Such Beauty and such wonder
Reaching into ugliness and shame?

Ha! The stupid sheep would find a better pasture?
The silly coin dropped in a dusty corner?
A foolish son to free-lance to disaster?
The dirty, disreputable, plastered in crime and rot?
Who cares? (Keep our distance! Disdain! Destroy!)

Like shepherd, woman, father,
God, not serenely pleased with all the righteous,
Nor basking in the praise of the unblemished good.
Yearns for, searches, reaches, to comfort and restore.
The longed-for lost.

And then, when found, a festival of joy.
A celebration of delight.
Back in the fold, the bleating sheep.
Back in the headband, the missing coin.
Back in the family, the wandering son.

Have we not also strayed
    From the goodness God supplied?
Have we not all transgressed against the holy will,
Squandering our heritage on this blessed earth?
Even to us, besmirched, bemired in dust,
Separated from our heaven-built home.

God our Father came,
Through storm, through wilderness terrain
Inviting, in eager waiting for our glad return
To the beauty of our home.
To the love where we belong.

Who Is Your Master?
(Luke 16:10-15; Matthew 06:24)

We "cannot serve God and mammon?"
Well, we keep on trying to.

Serving two masters!
We think we can!
One on Sunday, another on Monday.
One in the church, another in town, at home, or market place.
We really hate the one and love the other.

To which are we devoted?
To which do we give a passing nod
Or secretly despise, or openly disdain?

God is jealous.
Demanding all or none.
Mammon enslaves its subjects.
God frees His loyal servants.
We are His or none of His.

We Enter Now Your Kingdom
(Luke 16:16)

Kingdom of God!

Lord, help us to understand!
Your will, not ours to bend our way.
Your rule, not ours to frame you in.

Lord, give to us the earnest zeal
That we - May push beyond all laxity, excuse.
Give us the joyful strength
That we - May force aside all blockage to our faith,
That we - Resolute, and bold, may grasp the cross,
That we - May enter now your realm
      You have prepared and called us to.

Greatness
(Luke 16:19-31)

Surely I am special!

Did not the Lord choose me?
Others too, of course, but *me*!
I stand out, don't I?

What child is this?
In Jesus' arms
A simple child, open-eyed
Humility. Trusting.
Of such is the kingdom of God.

Who did not know Dives.
His great house, his luxury?
Who (besides dogs of the street)
Knew Lazarus?
Now in the bosom of Abraham.
Where is Dives?

Search for the great ones.
Ah, there, there they are,
Serving the "unimportant people",
The stranger, hungry, the sick,
In unsavory places,
In unrespectable unacceptable places.
In prisons, bedlam, in ugly circumstance.
There! There faith is found.
Where Jesus walks, touches, blesses.

Your Servants
(Luke 17:7-19)

You who have healed us
    From our uncleanness.

How can we praise you?
    You are our gladness.

You truly our master.
    We, surely, your servants.

Totally yours
    To do your good will.

No breaks from your service
    Because you are with us.

We've nothing to boast of
    You are our glory!

Who God Justifies
(Luke 18:9-14, 19:1-10)

See that man?

The one standing tall beside the temple wall.
Good man!
Keeps all the rules. Does more, besides.
Never gave his father any trouble.
Confident in himself, he doesn't beg of God for help.
No siree!
Thanks God that he is what he is.
Commands the people's respect.
Thanks God he belongs to a chosen people.
Better than the common crowd,
    Those on the other side of town.
        On the other side of the law,
            On the other side of well-behaved society.
                On the other side of the sea.
God could do with a few more men like him.

Oh. That other man?
The one crouching by the temple steps?
What a rot!
What right has he to pray to God?
The scamp! His family's black sheep.
Dishonest crook! Stole the people's money.
Despicable!
God could do with fewer men like him.

    He is weeping over his wrongdoing.
"God be merciful!", he cries
    Penitent, contrite, relies
    Not on himself, foresworn,
    Unpretentious, sobbing, he sighs,

        Kyrie! Eleison!

    (Riddle: Which man is justified by God?)
    (Test question: Why?)

A Few Words about a Little Man
(Luke 19:1-10)

They called him Zacchaeus
He never was pious.
He lived by ill-gotten gain.

He climbed up a tree
In order to see
This Jesus. He'd heard of His fame.

"Zacchaeus, come down!"
In Jericho town.
This evening the Lord is your guest.

"Half my goods to the poor.
What I've robbed I'll restore."
Zach offered to God all his best.

His zeal to get gold
Turned to zeal for the Lord.

Now he had but one goal.
To fulfill holy will.

As you saw, Lord, Zacchaeus,
Will You also, Lord, see us?

The Missing Covenant
(Luke 19:41-42; John 14:18-21)

The people of Judah, they wondered why,
Why the covenant had been broken!

Because beloved you did not heed it.
Though God chose you, you chose yourselves.
You went your way, to sate your lusts.
Instead of God you served your greed.
You broke your faith, kindled my wrath.
Yet my faith held, my love remained.
A brand new covenant I'll give you.
Engrave it on your finite heart.
And seal it with the blood of life
Of my anointed, special one.

The Christ-believers, they wondered why,
Why He God's sent divine reflection
Living among them, suffering, dying
Rising from death, conquering hate
Had gone and not returned to bless them!

"Where is your faith that moves the mountains?
Where is my spirit, sent to guide you?
Where is the love I left to bind you?
Where is the covenant I brought you?"

"Listen again, the Good News, the story!
Receive in your hearts His grace and His glory!"

*Jeremiah 31:31-34

Barabbas
(Luke 23:18-25)

When it comes to time's crises
> Whom do we choose?
> Brigand Barabbas?
>> Or the king of the Jews?

Every day's choices,
> Every day's strife
Are gateways to death
> Or portals to life.

>> The priest gave his verdict,
>>> Stood, crying aloud
>> His anger supported
>>> By the murmuring crowd.

We are scattered, or hiding,
> To save our own skins.
We flee from our Savior
> Taking shelter in our sins.

Oh, Jesus, we've seen Thee
> Healing sick and the blind.
Oh, Master, we'll follow
> Nor lag far behind.

>> We beg, let us join Thee
>>> To whom we belong
>> Nor ever desert Thee
>>> Our Joy and our Song.

Gospel Postscript
(Luke 24:13-35)

"Stay with us, friend stranger!
Stay with us, break bread, still with us abiding."

He remained for a moment,
Broke bread and blessed God's presence.

Then we knew Him…
How our lives were enlightened,
Our hopes freshly brightened.
With faith, now rejoicing,
We rose up, quick returning
To tell all the story:
"He lives, He forever!
Christ's love has restored us."

CHAPTER 4

BOOK OF JOHN

Thank You, John
(The Gospel according to John)

𝕵ohn?

John, reporter of the message,
Were we forgetful of its meaning?

Of gods and goddesses there are plenty,
We need no Jesus added to them,
Transient celebrities over whom we fawn.
We need no secret sacred knowledge,
No mystery religion or esoteric rites
Hid from the humble, credulous masses.

Jesus clearly spoke His counsel (as you tell us),
Not as His own, but words from the heavenly Father,
That He might pass them on in earnest urgency to chosen friends.

Sent by His Father, His life's full purpose was the Father's will,
Sent when the Day had come,
When the hour of full creation was approached,
Life of the ages, He brought an open invitation
To all people who give to Him their trust,
Who put their faith and hope in undoubting expectation
And in each moment's pulse of holy Love's expression
Of the ultimate glory, the completion of time's universal event.

> This is the message, John, you remind us;
> This is the union,
> The hallowed intertwined, the Father planter of the vine,
> The vine that nourishes the branch
> That furnishes the fruit that feeds the multitude.

> This is the message, John, that you remind us,
> The creature companied with Christ,
> The Spirit's Truth, Called-along-side
> The soul that breathes the Breath of God,

Everlasting Joy, forever!

Jesus
(The Gospel of John)

It's about a crucifixion
>What it was
>>What it did.

Creator enwrapped with creature,
A conflagration of distress and pain,
The ultimate of passion, refusal to disdain
The fleeting instants that would seek to stain
The bright and pure, ever-incessant flame,
The holy Self-surrender, prevailing and sustained,
The Breath unquenchable that breathes
Into the cosmic dust, the perfect realm of Light.

Such love
He gave
Such love believe
Such love to ever live.

Ah, Radiance from above,
Regenerate, renew us
>In thy *truth..*

Prologue to the Gospel of John
(John 01:1-5)

He came and He went
The ultimate event
For always He was
From Him who was sent
Was the sender because
He was the cause
And *His* was the cause
Spoken and heard
The infinite word.

Alive with His life
The essence expressed
The branch in the vine
The eternal compressed
And the life is the light
Illumining life
And that life: the love
Perfection in time.

The Messiah Is Found
(John 01:29-51)

They looked up at Him on whom their Teacher gazed.

Who was He, what was He
Whose appearance sent some unnamed thrill rippling through their souls?
They followed where He went,
Abiding where He stayed,
Calling on those they knew, to say:
    "We have found Him Whom we sought!"

Listen –
"Truly, truly, I say to you…"
    He spoke the *word* of Life
He spoke the *what* He was
    He was the *life* He lived.

    Amen! Amen!

The Call to Follow
(John 01:43-51)

Jesus said to Philip: "Follow me!"

Philip said to Nathanael: "Come and see!"
Nathanael under the fig tree,
Sceptic, scorned old Nazareth.

But when he saw, this Jesus,
"Son of God! King of Israel!"
Full of faith, lived in Love,
Trusting and triumphant—

Christ, I have come; I see You,
Lord, I follow. Lead and teach me.

Waiting His Word, Willing His Will
(John 02:3-4, 5:19, 7:3-6, 10:23-11:6)

"Jesus walked in the temple in Solomon's porch."

I am not independent.
I am not my own.
I am His, He who sent me,
To do my Father's will.

My family advise me.
My friends, they who call me,
The sick, they who need me.
I ponder, consider.

My companions, they warn me.
My enemies scorn me.
They threaten to stone me.
They challenge my works.

No move will I make,
No word will I say
Till the Father speaks to me
Till His Spirit flows through me.

I will wait for His Word.
I will will His good will.
I will walk while it's day.
Till my hour is come.

For my Father is near me
Beside me to hear me.
He speaks and I listen.
His intent stirs within me.

My Father, I obey Thee.
No fear will delay me.
Your purpose will guide me
"I and my Father are one."

Nicodemus
(John 03:1-20)

He came for a comment on law-keeping;
He heard a word, a whisper stirred,
A breeze of grace, of new living.

As a teacher of Israel, of God's mercy,
Instructor on God's will, on His Kingdom,
"Observe," he said, "minutely God's order.
Keep the Rules, the regulating tool of God's purpose.
Obey God," repeats Nicodemus.

"How obey God?" was always the question.
"Understand what is His measure,
Learn and keep His commandment."

"Repent your wrong! Practice paradise,
Perfect and purify.
Otherwise God may condemn you.
Other ways God may direct you."

"So, Rabbi,
How achieve the Messiah's redemption?"

"You can't blow the Wind," says the Lord.
"It is Wind that does the blowing.
New birth is new life that blazes with Love.
God's Wind is His Love,
The Breath of His Spirit."

Snapshots in Samaria
(John 04:7-42)

Religious trivia!
   She seeks escape
      in chatter.
God desires caring.

   Sad she comes alone.
      With joy returns
         with neighbors.
   Jesus at the well.

      Pure, cool, fresh water.
         Who can draw it
            from the deep?
      Love's living fountain.

      "Rabbi, eat," they said.
         Food He had they
            knew not of:
      God the Father's Will.

      Not where or when
      Or now and then.
      "The hour comes"
      Spirit and Truth.

There Came a Woman (of Samaria)
(John 04:7-45)

She didn't belong.

Rejected, discarded, despised.
Wrong?
She came to the well
Alone.

By the well a stranger sat.
Yes, even a Jew.
Hated?
She knew.

He broke the rule.
He spoke like a fool.
Asked:
"Give me a drink!"

She teased His thirst,
With mocking cursed
With ridicules.
Who would draw water without tools?

He offered to share
With genuine care.
Fresh Living Water, everlasting and sure,
Worship in Spirit, Holy Breath, truly pure.

Forgetting her pitcher, forgetting her fear,
Back to the village, "Come and hear
A prophet who knew all I have done,
A teacher who showed me a hope to be won."

At the Sheep Gate
(John 05:1-5)

At the Sheep Gate
And the stench of Hell
Where helplessness bleats
And suffering greets,
I heard a gentle voice,
A soft, offering choice,
"Do you want to get well?"
At the Sheep Gate.

How do I perceive the people passing by?
As pestilent passions of mortal misbehavior?
Unfortunate expressions of pain, human distress?

Do I stop for a moment to fathom Nature's Sorrow?
Or do I hasten from it quickly, cleanly, discreet,
Maybe post a prohibition preventing indiscretions
In defense of morals, despising petty quarrels?

How do I know His anguish, ignored, disdained
    His agony?
Can I describe His misery, His guilt, His stain's extremity?

Pause! Pause from my busyness! Speak to His present need.
A word say for encouragement: A word:
"Stand up. Trust. Proceed on the path God does provide,
The way Providence enables you in His Spirit, by His side!"

The Father Loves The Son
(John 05:19-26)

The Father loves the Son
    And shows Him all He does,
        That the Son may do them, too.
Remarkable, amazing, and greater things to do,
The goodness, the gladness, and the glory of our God.

Consider the nights of prayer,
    The early morning share.
It was thus He understood,
As the only Son, He would,
The nature He saw, He heard.
The wisdom of the word.

This is holy delight.
Immeasurable in might.

This is eternal life.
The Father loves the Son
And in that love we live.

"Thou art all we have
In the land of the here, of the living,"
The grace, the gift, the forgiving,
    Thou art all we have.

"In the morning we know Thy love.
We put our trust in Thy being.
Show us the way we must take,"
Till the evening we know Thy love.*

*Psalm 142:5-6a, 143:8

Testimony
(John 05:32-47)

The man who knew Him

The God who loved Him
The Word that spoke Him
The Lord of Life.

He is Who knows us
It is He loves us
His word speaks to us
Eternal Life.

By Himself
(John 06:15)

He withdrew by himself to the hills.
All of God was in His soul.

He withdrew by himself to pray.
All the world was in His heart.

The Foolish Crowd
(John 06:1-15)

They sought Him because they saw His healings.

They sought Him for the plenteous food He fed them.
    But they didn't understand.
    They really didn't understand.
They came to Him, they thought to make Him king:
He was for them a wonder-working thing.
    But they didn't understand.
They thought He'd tool for them their pleasure,
      Give them pride,
      Give them power,
      Give them glory.
They'd rule over fools
      With follies pushed aside.
Enjoy prosperity's unmitigated measure.

And so He left them,
    Returning to His holy place of prayer.

They didn't understand. They couldn't understand
His great compassion nor His heart of love.

Afraid?
(John 06:16-21)

There is a story about some people who were afraid.

That is why they saw mystery in solid sense.
They saw a ghost in goodness. They trembled in the night.
They were frightened at the sight
Of their dearest friend, they would let him pass them by.

They fled from hope.

Oh, folk of faltering faith,
In storm and stress, self-bound distress,
You fail the courage you possess,
Gift of your calling you forget.

And yet
His presence in the dark
Is like the light of truth, His voiced assurance:
"I am here, be not afraid."

Oh, joyful comfort, come aboard, come and stay.
The wind winds down.
The waves subside.
We are home, for YOU are here.
And YOU, you say:
"I AM with you."
    We will not fear.

This is our story, no longer afraid.
Our faith is in God. We trust in His goodness.
We are glad through the night, through the tempests of life.
Heaven's light goes before us, it will not pass us by.

Our hope is in God. He is with us.

Disciples' Prayer
(John 06:27-40)

Thine is the life for which we thirst and hunger,

The drink, the bread, the daily nourishment,
The feast of fellowship, the food of faith;
The merriment responding to thine eternal spirit,
Obedient in grace, radiant in Thy mercy
With the deep, unfailing joy we name salvation,
The call, the claim, the ultimate event,
Eternal life, our God's divine intent.

Though pinned with the pain of Thy creation's cross,
It is the cross of love, the self lost in the gift
Of holy kindness. Lift, we pray,
Our souls to Thy plane where we may share,
Partaking, distributing, the nature of Thy will.

Divine Intent
(John 07:3-35)

CHRIST, GOD'S PURPOSE, PREVAILS.
Man may interfere with it
To prevent it and defeat it,
Intrude in it with his own pretty plans,
Build temples,
    Raise his towers,
        Forge his little kingdoms.
These all quickly disappear.
They roll away in dust,
Moth-eaten, corroded with rust
Of forgotten time.

God's purpose, however, still prevails.
They who believe in it,
    Who love it
        And receive it,
They partake of it, of God's perfecting purpose.
They will His perfect will,
They work His full intent
Compulsion of delight,
Eternity in sight.

Are You Blind?
(John 09:39-41)

Do you understand?
>Come to JESUS.
>Learn of Him
>As His disciples.
>Then you will know, you, the blind
>Who lead the blind.

"COME to Jesus. And believe. He will open your eyes. You will see."

(Conversation ended.
>They went away, preferring blindness,
Undazzled in the darkness, by the Light of the World.)

Sin No More
(John 08:1-11)

The sinner condemns.
   The Savior redeems.
Condemnation destroys.
   Redemption restores.

     She was, so we,
         Temptation's slave.
     God's charity
         Would make her brave.
     No more condemned,
         No more in shame,
     From sin unhemmed,
         Freed by God's claim.

Truth

(John 08:39-47; 17; 18:37-38)

(This is drawn from Jesus' conversation with the Pharisees and from His conversation with the Governor Pilate and from His prayer for the disciples.)

𝕿*ruth*, you see. We do not understand.
    The high priests did not understand.
        They ruled to hold their rule.
            Pilate did not understand.
                His politics were politics of power.
Jesus explained: "My kingship is not of this world...
        I have come to bear witness to the truth."

      What is truth?
"Your Father, the devil, he was a murderer.
In the Truth he is not
Because not is Truth in him."

The way we live, conduct ourselves, and what we live by
Are determined by our active response
To the demonic
Or to divine reality.

No, we do not understand this Jesus
Except that He maddens us, or delights.
We must rid ourselves of Him or glorify Him
    In whose glory we glory.

In Him we see, by His life, by all He did and taught
The Reality of God.
Now if we live by this, if we trust it,
Conduct our lives by it, by this revelation
Of Godly goodness: This is the truth.

One Thing I Know!
(John 09)

𝕳e passed by. I did not see Him. He saw me. Stopped. Cared.

Hey, blind man, what happened to you?
You used to sit all day, and doleful, by your beggar's cup.
You used to…
Why, you *see! You see?*
Blind from birth. You cannot see!
See! Your once-dead eyes, now lively, bright.

Who? Who opened your eyes?

"Don't know.
 Yes, I *do*. Name's *Jesus*."

How? How did He?

"Don't know.
 Yes…! Yes, I *do*.
He put spittle, spit with common clay, smeared on my eyes".
He said, "Go. Wash in the pool of Siloam (means Sent)."
I went,
Washed,
Saw,
Saw, I tell you.

"Come back with me,
 And see, Jesus."

Where? Where is He?

"Don't know.
 Yes…! Yes, I *do*.
Near me. Beside me. See!"

Continued

Really?
Come now. Tell the men of religion.
They'll know.

"Pharisees? They don't know."
Called by parents for proof.
    They didn't know.
    Afraid, they were. Timid. Get into trouble.
"Ask him," they said, pointing to me
"He's of age," they said. "he can speak for himself."
(I, the sinner, teaching the teachers!)
They asked me: "Who? How? Where? What? Is He?"
They wouldn't believe.
(You have to believe.)
Such blabber: "Jesus," they said, "is a sinner.
    He couldn't help you."
"Jesus," I said, "is a prophet.
    He helped me."

"One thing I know," I assured them:
"I was blind. Now I see. Jesus!"

Jesus Wept
(John 11:35)

Why do you weep, my Lord,
    And wherefore your sorrow?
You once told us stories, Lord,
    Of God's will for tomorrow.

Your welcome's not cheap, sir King.
    Your *love's* no soft pillow.
You showed us earth's glories, King,
    Of lily and willow.

Your pathways are steep, our Lord,
    The gateway is narrow.
Your compassion is broad, Lord,
    For the reed and the sparrow.*

*Psalm 102:7 – KJV, Luke 12:6

End Days
(John 11:47-57)

The elders in the council chambers plotting "How to kill Him?"

The curious crowd in the temple court in gossip. "Is He coming?'

Disciples in a roadside town praying "How to love them?"

How do we pass our end of time? "Self-serving or self-giving?"

Or if we live by, responding to, all
That is deceitful, false, evil, - well
That is the evil, controls our lives,
Determines how we live.
Choose.

That Day
(John 13:34-36, 14:20, 15:12-17, 16:5)

*L*ove, divine self-giving,

God, the Father, through Christ (so we call the Creative Word)
Planned, purposed, prepared from the very beginning,
The New,
Now in its fulfilling,
The atmosphere designed,
The life-breath of the Ultimate:
This is *that day*
For which we were chosen, called, awakened.
(From which we can turn, of course, away, sleep away
Or which we can accept and enter, the medium of *that* Blessed *day*).

The "new commandment" of *that day* is the living principle
Of the New Life. That is: to "love one another" is
The nature of the new creation,
The freshness of the new and everlasting beginning.
When this overwhelming *love* is released.

This *that day* when the disciple is filled with *love*
And guided by it in all his actions.
It is the spontaneous relationship of those
Who have received it from God through their fellowship with Christ.

That day we live in *love*.

Yet A Little While
(John 14:19, 16:16-19)

...Catch our breath!...
    ...It's about to happen...
        From the other side of the hill (good? or bad?)!
Isaiah warned of Assyrians...
Jeremiah of Babylon...
Unwarned, a sudden approaching
    Onrushing.
What will it do when it meets us?
Will we recoil when it comes
And the whirlwind whips the moment's little while?

"Yet a little while the world will not see me," He said.
"Will *we*?"

His Word
(John 14:10, 18, 19:23-26, 30)

His word was never subject
To the stumbling language of our frozen phrases,
Nor framed to fit our private prejudices, our creeds, our crude Christologies
Of a god formed from our phantasies, a messiah spun out of our dreams.

Rather it was and now remains the winged Spirit of eternal truth
That flies us not away into the emptiness of space
But flies us into the midst of life where we,
Like Him, submit to the scourging
The world's wild, wanton will would inflict upon and in us.
As though to frighten us, discourage us from the witness of God's love,
Enduring, patient, long-suffering, caring grace,
Bold enemies of the temporal conflicts of self-centered shame.

His Word is a witness to the everness of faith.
His Word is the secret of the whereabouts of hope.
His Word is the definition of demonstrated Love.
His Word whispers to us the syllables of joy we share.
His Word is the laughter that peals away time's pain.
His Word is the bond that binds us, brings us into peace.
His Word is the word that glows with a radiating light.
    For the world is right when His Word is light
        And His light is the life of creation.

The Commandment's Commission
(John 14:25:31)

He would leave us,
    But not orphans.
He would give us
    One beside us.

To teach, and guide us,
    Sacred Presence,
Comfort, Counsel,
    Hope's reminder.

We shall live
    For He lives in us.
Come, Lord Jesus,
    Come, Christ's Father.

Help us know,
    Keep your commandments,
Love You, Lord,
    And Love Your Father,
Love each other,
    Co-sojourners.

Come, Friend Jesus,
    Come, our Father
And dwell with us,
    Take possession.

Use us, send us,
    Your disciples
Your Word speaking,
    Live it through us.

Connection
(John 15:1-11)

*A*h!

This is the faith!
This is home. This is where we live,
    Where we work,
    Where we rejoice, converse,
Making merry, learning, loving, with our family:

Abiding!
    With Christ our comrade,
    With God, our Father.

        We with Him. He with us.
        That is how we produce together.
        What He has done we do.
        What He has said we share.
        We ask for His help as we labor.
    He helps what we do for His glory.

Our Father, our Comrade, companions,
Bonded in Love, our home's haven,
His command is our common endeavor,
Our joyful joint reason for being.
Our delight, an eternal attachment,
A daily glad, glowing enrichment
Continuing, dwelling, remaining.

Always

Abiding!
In His word, in His love, abiding.

You Are My Friends
(John 15:14-15)

You see Him who is standing high on the windswept hillside
Talking to the listening crowd
Who press forward to catch His every word!

You see Him mingling among the people
Touching the eyes of the blind,
Pressing the crumbling hands of the leper,
Looking lovingly in the wondering eyes of a child!

He is my friend, or so He said He would be
If I were impulsed by His love,
Moved by His deep compassion,
Infected by His will.

The First Day
(John 20:1)

They slept.
And many never knew
To the day of their death
What they missed that morning.

We sleep.
And from birth to death
We may never come to know
What we've lost in living.

Do You Not Know That I Have Power?
(John 18:36-37; 19:10, 22)

The accoutrements of power:

The pride of prestige quickly passed
As a flash of sunlight
Clouded by a squandered squall of rain,
Forgotten now like last night's headache
    After the party's vapid strain.

Who was He? So who would know,
Written in the records that His brief reign
Occurred awhile when Love walked barefoot
In stony streets, by rubbish heaps, by cots of pain
    To care, restore, encourage…

That then when arrested and suppressed,
Lest it make too clear for conscience
The gentle force of kindness,
He was tortured, torn from time and crucified.
    And thus He lives forever.

Who did you say was king?

CHAPTER 5

RANDOM THOUGHTS

The Synoptic Gospels – I

How is it,
We, being human
In various parts of the earth
    (Sun's satellite in finiteless universe),
In various points of history
Who variously encode our understandings,
Yet focus, flash, on one brief fused chronology,
One poignant flame of life
Flushed from agony of birth,
Formed in a fellowship of faith
By which new being forms?

How is it
That this, the "GOSPEL"
(Fleet yet enduring happy news)
Proclaimed one very short time
About one brief life lived among a very few,
Back ways of civilization, some may say,
Appointed to be
Gospel of love.
Anointed of God,
To meet, to mean,
    Infinity?

The Synoptic Gospels – II

Jesus? Jesus? Who was Jesus?

What did He do?
What did He say?
    This long-ago Jew?
Maybe it was deeper than ever we knew?
What He did, what He said, was in sum what He was.
And what He was, was in substance
The word of creation,
The worth of existence,
The meaning of being,
The window for seeing
The goal of perfection,
Love's rich expression,
Self-giving, enabling,
Divine, holy presence
Hope in fulfillment.
Faith's full allegiance.

Jesus? This Jesus?
Who is this Jesus?
Our friend, comrade, master.
He called us,
We with Him,
To the great congregation.
We bring them
Home with us
To the house of His Father.

Tabernacled Questions

$\mathfrak{A}$re we God's people
    Chosen and called for?
        Gathered and guided?
Where did we come from?
Where are we going?
    Why?

And what are we here for,
    Fumbling and grumbling
    Complaining and straining
    For the water of life,
    In the wilderness?

Are we God's people?

Templed Questions

$\mathfrak{W}$here is this Messiah
(Foretold by Isaiah)
Friend or false prophet?
Hush! Unsafe and improper
To mention or talk of!

Yet look! He's now speaking
By the wall of the temple.
By the tall temple tower.
He's the one we are seeking?
A new way He's teaching.
Beyond law love is reaching.

Tabernacle and Temple

$\mathfrak{W}$hat are we here for?
Perhaps to listen and to live out His message,
To act out His counsel and to work by His purpose,
To walk by His spirit.

The Via Dolorosa

Where will Love take me
    If I follow the cross?

If I watch from safe distance
    Would I know the persistence
    Of Love, fully given,
        If I follow the cross?

Or would Love awake me
    From my indolent slumber
    That I might discover
        The way of the cross?

Would heaven escape me,
    Friends, fellows forsake me
    If I follow the cross?

Would His enemies make me
    Bear His pain and His passion
        If I follow the cross?

Where will Love take me?
    Mid the scourgers and scoffers,
    The proud earth-oppressors,
    Or the crowds Christ would sigh for,
    The sinners He would die for
        If I follow the cross?

Where will Love take me?
    Where there's light for the shadows,
    Healing for time's sorrows
    Hope in God's tomorrows
        If I follow the cross.

With Christ, Love would take me
    In His selfless compassion
        If I follow the cross.

Hesed (Chesedh)

There was a word the ancient Hebrews used for relationships.

It meant attraction, respect, kindness, caring, faithfulness between people.
It had a special meaning when used of God in His relationship
with His people.
As such it is found mostly in the Psalms, the hymns and poetry of faith.
But it is also found in the "Prophets."
What is that special meaning?
For 300 years translators used the English word "loving-kindness,"
And some used the word "mercy."
And later, others used the words "steadfast love."
Another translation was "unfailing love,"
Or even "persistent love."
But always there was "love,"
And always that "love" was "faithful."
It was used in the context of "covenant."
God gave a "covenant" to His chosen people.
He would take care of them, but they must be true to Him;
          They must be true to each other.
Again and again they failed their part of the bargain:
 They abused God's goodness, they misused their neighbors.
But God was faithful—and God is faithful—to His part.
That is His loving-kindness: it is steadfast;
It is unfailing, ever persistent love.
Not a sentimental love! Not indulgent love! Not permissive love!
But a persistent, caring, even suffering love.

That was the way the Psalmist felt about the wonder of God's love.
That was how the Prophets understood God's suffering
When His people, wayward, went astray,
 Unfaithful, unresponding to His love.

 Can we claim to be God's people?
 Do we sense His steadfast love?
 Are we true to Him and faithful?
 Do we love God's love for neighbor?

Riddle From the Gospels

What happened then? Is happening? And still will happen?

We see the glimmering of its past, but also we
    See it blossoming in the Eastern's near horizon.

If we turn toward it, watch, and listen
It comes to us and, if we allow,
    It captures and compels us,
    Projects us and propels us,
    Invites us and involves us
    In unending Universe.

It is a Word
    Whispered
        In the secret corner of the heart
            Yet rolling like cascading thunder through the cosmos.

If we seek to define it, we lose it.
But, defined by it, we are found

        And the Found is Love and Lives.

Thoughts on the Lord's Prayer

Prayer is reaching out to God who is more.

Prayer is contact with God
Christian prayer is conversation with God.
It is directing our thoughts to God.
God, not ourselves, is the center of our attention
God is our Father, we come to Him as His children
God is not just my Father, nor just your Father
    But ours together
God, our Father, is greater than all His creation,
       Than all His creatures.
He is above all.
We have a request to make of God, our Father.
It is the primary yearning of the Christian disciple.
It is a request that in His realm, His rule
His purpose for all His creatures
       Be realized. His kingdom come.
Not that our individual wishes,
       But that His will be done.
In the perfection of heaven God's will is perfectly done.
We yearn that it be perfectly done on Earth,
       Among us, in our times.

"Feed us," we pray, "with the bread of life
That we might live by faith, trusting,
For today, and for God's tomorrow."

One Will Come

In a time of stress,
In a time of despair and distress,
Yet of desire anticipating change
To peace and happiness!
"One will come!" they whispered,
"Will one come?" they wondered.

Out of the wilderness
Like a dark cloud of thunder
Like a bright sky of promise
Came a herald, a cry:

"One will come!
He is already here. See?
Already one comes
As a thresher comes
To free the wheat from the chaff,
To purge the weed from the lily.
So beware! Turn from the dusk of your shadows.
Rejoice! Turn toward the dawn of His radiance!"

Neighbor

How may I attain eternal life?

Love God.
Love your neighbor as yourself.

Who is my neighbor?
He who, on meeting misery,
    Responds with immediate mercy.
She who, on seeing suffering,
    Reacts with unquestioning kindness.
Who does not count the cost
    Nor rate the risk,
But with spontaneous caring comes to help
With an inbred attitude of fellow-feeling,
With an inborn habit of tenderness.

Blessed are the merciful!

Am I a neighbor?

Martha, Mary

No one need make up this tale.
No need to suit some teaching, like a parable.

A passing incident remembered,
    A casual remark of rich significance.

It was not that Martha had so much to do.
It was that she was 'troubled' by them.
They were her pressuring priorities.

It was not that Mary had nothing else to do.
It was only that to listen, learn, at the master's feet
Took all precedence. God's present evidence.

To toil at tasks; a busyness, a fretting for her guest
    Was Martha's attentive stress.

To harken, heed, to hang on words the guest would say
    Was Mary's chief concern.

After all and above all—
How often does awaking wisdom come our way?
How frequently does holy love and joy enter our home?

May we then choose the better part.

(It could be a time to be burdened with the crush of life!
Or could be a time to be yoked to the love of Christ!
    Mary chose the better part.)

Jesus Wonders

Who knows the thoughts of the boy, Jesus,
Growing up, attending the synagogue,
Reading the law and the prophets and the writings,
Hearing the comments of the Rabbis
Pondering them,
Seeing about Him and hearing
A people and a practice not in accord with God's word?
Who knows what the Man, Jesus, thought,
Working in the carpenter shop,
Talking with His fellows, listening.

Something must be done. Who would do it?
The Messiah would do it!
For Him the people were waiting.
He would make everything right.
But why wait? Was the law not already known?
Had God not spoken through His poets and prophets?
Was the time of fulfillment not now?
Why wait?

When He went with the crowds to the Jordan to be baptized,
When He walked into the wilderness alone,
Something must be done and He knew it. Who would do it?
God had put His spirit upon Him. God had anointed Him.

Continued

But how would He do it?
Ah, the power of faith! He could do it!
But His body, weak needed food.
He could turn stones into bread.
He, unknown, was a peasant, a nobody.
Ah! He could throw himself from the temple.
The crowds would marvel, listen, believe.
Ah! He could become great,
    In God's name He could own the world,
        Enforce Righteousness.

He rejected the way of man, self-interest,
Of celebrity, attention-getting,
Or the violent path to power.

Back He came to the people,
    To walk God's way among them.

        To be rejected!

Scripture Index

Habakkuk 03:19 **26**

Isaiah 05:1-7 **36**

Jeremiah 12:7 **36**
Jeremiah 31:31-34 **101**
John **106, 107**
John 01:1-5 **108**
John 01:29-51 **109**
John 01:43-51 **109**
John 01:6-7 **14**
John 02:3-4, 5:19, 7:3-6, 10:23-11:6 **110**
John 03:1-20 **111**
John 03:2-3 **16**
John 04:7-42 **112**
John 04:7-45 **113**
John 05:1-5 **114**
John 05:19-26 **115**
John 05:32-47 **116**
John 06:1-15 **117**
John 06:15 **116**
John 06:16-21 **118**
John 06:27-40 **119**
John 07:3-35 **120**
John 08:1-11 **122**
John 08:39-47; 17; 18:37-38 **123**
John 09 **124**
John 09:39-41 **121**
John 11:35 **126**
John 11:47-57 **127**
John 12:12-15 **59**
John 12:27 **91**
John 13:34-36, 14:20, 15:12-17, 16:5 **128**
John 14:10, 18, 19:23-26, 30 **130**
John 14:18-21 **101**
John 14:19, 16:16-19 **129**
John 14:25:31 **131**
John 15:1-11 **132**
John 15:14-15 **133**
John 18:36-37; 19:10, 22 **134**
John 19:25-30 **70**
John 20:1 **133**
John 20:1-18 **71**
John 20:17 **83**

Luke 02:25-38 **16, 74**
Luke 02:8-15 **12**
Luke 04:16-30 **53**
Luke 05:12-16 **75**
Luke 06:12-13 **28**
Luke 06:12-16, 9:1-6 **76**
Luke 06:20-49 **17**
Luke 06:41-42 **25**
Luke 09:1-6, 10, 22-26, 12:32-34 **77**
Luke 09:57-62 **45**
Luke 10:1-9, 16-17 **79**
Luke 10:27 **80**
Luke 11:1 **82**
Luke 11:1-4 **81**
Luke 11:14-12:4 **84**
Luke 11:14-26 **84**
Luke 11:2 **83**
Luke 11:29-36 **85**
Luke 11:37-41 **86**
Luke 11:42-52 **87**
Luke 11:53-54 **49**
Luke 12:1 **88**
Luke 12:22-34 **23**
Luke 12:4-12 **90**
Luke 12:4-48 **89**
Luke 12:6 **126**
Luke 13:34-35, 19:41 **91**
Luke 13:34-39 **36**
Luke 13:41-56, 17:20-37 **92**
Luke 14:15-35 **93**
Luke 15 **94**
Luke 16:10-15 **95**
Luke 16:16 **96**
Luke 16:19-31 **52, 97**
Luke 17:7-19 **98**
Luke 18:9-14, 19:1-10 **99**
Luke 19:1-10 **61, 100**
Luke 19:28-38 **59**
Luke 19:41-42 **101**
Luke 20:1-8 **60**
Luke 20:20-26 **34**
Luke 20:27-40 **63**
Luke 20:45-47 **65**
Luke 21:1-4 **66**

Luke 21:12-19 **68**
Luke 21:5-7 **66**
Luke 21:8-36 **67**
Luke 22:3-22 **42**
Luke 22:38-46 **69**
Luke 23:18-25 **102**
Luke 24:10-12 **71**
Luke 24:13-35 **103**

Mark 01:1-13 **44**
Mark 01:12-20 **27**
Mark 01:16-20 **45**
Mark 01:16-22 **46**
Mark 01:32-37 **47**
Mark 01:32-39 **48**
Mark 01:32-44 **49**
Mark 01:40-45 **75**
Mark 03:33-35 **50**
Mark 06:1-6 **53**
Mark 06:34 **51**
Mark 09:42; 11:22-23 **52**
Mark 10:1-16 **54**
Mark 10:17-31 **55**
Mark 10:32-52 **61**
Mark 11-12 **57**
Mark 11:1-10 **59**
Mark 11:27-33 **60**
Mark 12:13-17 **34**
Mark 12:18-27 **63**
Mark 12:28-31 **64**
Mark 12:29-31 **80**
Mark 12:37-40 **65**
Mark 12:41-44 **66**
Mark 13:1-4 **66**
Mark 13:5-37 **67**
Mark 13:9-13 **68**
Mark 14:10-18 **42**
Mark 14:32-42 **69**
Mark 15:24-33 **70**
Mark 16:1,9 **71**
Mathew 24:9-14 **68**
Matthew 02:1, 10, 11 **12**
Matthew 03:1-12 **14**
Matthew 03:1-3, 13-4:1 **13**
Matthew 03:13-4:1 **44**

Matthew 03:7-10 **15**
Matthew 04:17 **16**
Matthew 05-7 **17**
Matthew 05:1-12 **21**
Matthew 05:13 **18**
Matthew 06:19-34 **23**
Matthew 06:24 **95**
Matthew 06:5-15 **19**
Matthew 06:9-15 **21**
Matthew 07:1-5, 10:24-25 **25**
Matthew 07:13-20 **26**
Matthew 08:1-4 **75**
Matthew 08:19-22 **27**
Matthew 09:32-34 **84**
Matthew 10:28-33 **90**
Matthew 11:28-30 **28**
Matthew 13:10-15 **29**
Matthew 13:53-58 **53**
Matthew 17:1-8, 14-18 **30**
Matthew 18:21-35 **31**
Matthew 18:6-7 **52**
Matthew 19:30-20:16 **32**
Matthew 21:23-27 **60**
Matthew 22:1-14 **33**
Matthew 22:15-22 **34**
Matthew 22:23-33 **63**
Matthew 22:37-40 **80**
Matthew 23:1-36 **35, 65**
Matthew 23:13-37 **87**
Matthew 23:25-26 **86**
Matthew 23:37-39 **36, 91**
Matthew 24:1-3 **66**
Matthew 24:4-36 **67**
Matthew 25:1-13 **38**
Matthew 25:14-30 **39**
Matthew 25:31-46 **40, 41**
Matthew 26:14-25 **42**
Matthew 26:36-46 **69**
Matthew 27:39-49, 55-56 **70**
Matthew 28:1 **71**
Matthew 31:1-9 **59**
Matthew 6:9-13 **81**

Psalm 102:7 **126**
Psalm 142:5-6a, 143:8 **115**